AF660584

SOCIOLOGY OF AGING

About the Author

Prof. D.P. Saxena (*b.* 1934) obtained Master Degrees in Economics (1956) & Sociology (1959) and LL.B. degree (1957) from Agra University. He joined Department of Sociology, Gorakhpur University in 1959. Further he obtained Doctorate degree in Sociology from Gorakhpur University in 1967, on his research work on "Causes and Consequences of Rural Emigration in East U.P.". Later on he became Professor & Head, Sociology Department, Gorakhpur University. Besides teaching U.G. and P.G. classes in Sociology for about 35 years he supervised more than a dozen Doctoral research work on various socio-economic and cultural problems. He conducted a UGC Research Project on 'Rural Towns' in 1986. Another UGC Research Project on **"Sociology of Aging Among the Senior Citizens"** was conducted during 1998-2000 and its Final Report was submitted to the UGC in 2001.

Some of his papers on theoretical issues on sociology were published in national and international journals of Sociology. He is a life member of Indian Sociology Society (New Delhi), Indian Society of Criminology (Madras) and Indian Gerontological Association (BHU, Varanasi).

In the Annual Conference of Indian Sociological Society, he has been presenting for the last four years a status paper on "Sociology of Aging" under Research Committee No. 19 on "Age and Social Structure" of the Indian Sociological Society.

SOCIOLOGY OF AGING

D.P. Saxena

CONCEPT PUBLISHING COMPANY, NEW DELHI-110059

Cataloging in Publication Data—DK
Courtesy: D.K. Agencies (P) Ltd. <docinfo@dkagencies.com>

Saxena, D. P. (Dhirendra Prakash), 1934-
Sociology of aging / D.P. Saxena.
p. cm.
Study conducted in Gorakhpur City of Uttar Pradesh, India.
Includes bibliographical references.
Includes index.
ISBN 8180692728

1. Aging—India—Gorakhpur. 2. Older people—India—Gorakhpur—Social conditions. 3. Older people—India—Gorakhpur—Economic conditions. I. Title.

305.260 954 2 22

All rights reserved. No part of this work may be reproduced, stored in a retrieval system or transmitted in any form or by any means, electronic, mechanical, photocopying, microfilming, recording or otherwise, without the prior written permission of the copyright owner and the publisher.

ISBN : 81-8069-272-8

First Published 2006

© D.P. Saxena (*b.* 1934)

Published and Printed by
Ashok Kumar Mittal
Concept Publishing Company
A/15-16, Commercial Block, Mohan Garden,
New Delhi-110059 (India)
Phones : 25351460, 25351794
Fax : +91-11-25357103
Email : publishing@conceptpub.com

PREFACE

The present study is a comprehensive analysis of the patterns and processes of socio-economic and bio-psychological problems of aging and their adjustment among the senior citizens of four categories, viz. the superannuated University teachers, civil servants, elderly lawyers and doctors. The Sociological aspects of aging is concerned not only with changes in bio-psychological but also changes in the economic status and the position of the elderly as a member of the family, the community and the society. The changes and events associated with time include age grading and social attitudes and behaviour of the elderly as well as of the society in general towards the aging individuals. Further the Sociological perspective, the main thrust of the present study, considers not only how age may affect or impede the social functioning of the elderly but raises the question of how social factors affect the process of physical aging and other dimensions of aging in the society.

Old age is generally accompanied by a number of problems that the elderly have to face and adjust within varying degrees. These problems are mainly : insufficient income to support themselves and their dependents; ill health; no creative use of free time; less social security; lack of love and recognition; decreasing social participation; less dignity and self respect; loss of economic independence; declining physical vigour and the emergence of various types of degenerative diseases. All these consequences of aging change the elderly from the independent self-supporting individual to one who is now in need of help and shelter and requires help from his children, members of the family and the society in general. Further there are also typical myths about the aging individuals such as decline in their mental power, the loss of resistance to changes, forgetfulness, becoming cranky and difficult. In this respect scientists have discovered that mental power like problem solving, reaches its peak in later years of life. All this brings us to conclude that since aging is a normal process, we not only can equip ourselves to cope with it when it comes, but also enjoy the opportunities and challenges it presents. They can indeed, be as exciting and rewarding as those of our youth.

Acknowledgments

It is a matter of honour to express my deep sense of gratitude to Professor S.P. Nagendra, Former Vice Chancellor, Lucknow University and Head of the Department of Sociology, Gorakhpur University for his stimulating guidance, personal interest and constant encouragement.

This study would not have been possible but for the cooperation of my respondents of different categories, viz. superannuated University teachers, Civil servants, elderly lawyers and doctors who in spite of their old age and busy schedule of their medical and legal professional work, discussed their problems with me. I am very much obliged to all of them.

I am thankful to Professor P.V. Ramamurthy Director, Centre for Research on Aging, Department of Psychology, S.V. University, Tirupati for providing me all the facilities in the collection of vast information about various researches on Aging conducted at the Centre.

Behind every researcher there are number of Professors, colleagues and friends who provide invaluable support and assistance in the successful completion of the major research project. In this regard I wish to express my heart-felt gratitude to Professor Sheo Bahal Singh, Prof. P.S. Pandey, Professor G.B. Sahay and Mr. Manvendra Pratap Singh (Sociology Department, Gorakhpur University), Dr. Dharamvrat Tewari (Dept. of Distance Education, Gorakhpur University), Dr. B.P. Tripathi, M.B.B.S., Ex. President of G.P. Association, Gorakhpur, Dr. Seth (M.M. Nursing Home, Gorakhpur) and Mr. Awadhesh Kumar Srivastava, Senior Advocate, Ex. M.L.A. and President of Senior Citizen Forum, Gorakhpur for their untiring assistance in the collection of field data.

I would like to thank Chief Librarians of Tata Institute of Social Sciences, Deonar, Bombay, B.H.U., Varanasi and Gorakhpur University for the help rendered in the location of as well as making the research material on Aging available for the major research project with me.

I am also grateful to the President & Secretary of "Association of Gerontology (India), Varanasi" for enlightening me about many valuable and comprehensive findings of the researches on Aging conducted both in India and abroad and also providing me an opportunity for presenting a Research paper on 'Aging' at the International Conference on Aging organised at B.H.U. Campus, Varanasi from 7-9 November, 2000.

Lastly, I am much grateful to the Chairman, University Grants Commission, New Delhi for the necessary financial assistance in conducting the present major research project.

December 31, 2000 **D.P. Saxena**

CONTENTS

LIST OF TABLES

1 SOCIOLOGY OF AGING
Global Scenario and Indian Perspective

Introduction

The problem of aging among the senior citizens has a special significance in contemporary societies. In the traditional society of the past in India, the old age was no problem at all. Elderly persons were respected more than the younger ones. They were the chief patrons of the family. The stable joint family system in traditional Indian society was definitely a guarantee for the protection of the age. Initially under the regime of *laissez faire* the elderly people had to struggle hard to take care of their welfare and face the hazards of old age individually with their own efforts. There was none to look after their health and comfort due to acute non-availability of social security measures for the elderly people.

It is only since the advent of the Welfare State that every person irrespective of whether he was young or old, acquired the right among other things to live comfortably as a citizen of his country. Many social welfare and security legislations were enacted by the welfare State to safeguard the interests of the individual citizens. Some measures of social security for the old and the retired persons have no doubt come to exist in India but only these measures are not sufficient to redress the problems of aging of the senior citizens in the country. The lot of the elderly in India is changing rapidly with the increase in the population of senior citizens. In 1947 only 19 million people in the country were 60 plus. Today, more than 50 years later, the figure has risen to 70 million an increase of 50 million since independence. In the next 25 years the number of aged persons in India is projected to increase by 107 million by 2025. A large percentage of the aged are poor and destitute and bereft of even the basic necessities of life, namely food, shelter, clothing. The government endeavours to provide for this segment of society, but is limited by resource constraints. In this way along with an ever increasing longevity, the changing age profile of India's population has thrown up new problems faced by an aging population. This has become a matter of urgent social concern but remains under-researched.

There are some popular myths about old age. As regards meaning of 'the aged' the Department of Social Welfare of Maharashtra State brands 'The aged' as 'Apangas' (i.e. disabled) and clubs them with physically handicapped. The old people who were treated reverentially in primitive, preindustrial societies, existing in a Golden Age, are now much worse off in modern societies. They are being neglected by their families, forced into boring and meaningless retirement and derogated by the Youth culture.

The prestige accorded to the old broadly depends on the four components: Advisory, Contributory, Control and Residual. The first component comprises the greater experience of the old. The second arises from their participation in cultural, familial and economic activities. The control component arises from their possession of property, practical knowledge and experience what would be called the residual component depends on their previous status in their communities.

Acceptance of and consideration for the elderly varies according to cultural differences. In Japan in spite of development and modernization the old are respected whereas in India in spite of utter poverty, the old are looked upon with great deal of respect. They are considered to be mines of experience and knowledge. Younger people approach them for advice and guidance. It is very common among the Keralites to honour those who reach the age of 60 by celebrating '*Shasthipoorthi*'. The celebration is a symbol of reverence and respect accorded to the aged because they were once the part and parcel of the society and still they are.

The old in the past had exercised power because they owned and controlled property and had the freedom to dispose of this property. Wealth and property can be powerful weapons in the family and kinship system. Many elderly persons enjoyed attention and concern from their relatives as they kept them guessing about their last will and consciousness. It has been observed that people in most oriental cultures attach unique and special qualities to the old. Folk wisdom and social science indicate that age may be associated with characteristics that are positively valued by men like maturity, wisdom and spiritual and self-acceptance. Studies made by Gopelwar (1964), Manjula (1967), Narain (1979) and Nirmala (1969) show that family and kin still play an important role in providing economic, social and psychological security to the aged.

In developed societies too, differences are seen in the conditions of the old depending on various factors, such as old age, security measures, health care and cultural attitudes to the family. Though in highly developed Japan the old are here integrated into the family and community life, while in western societies, the old living away from the family are not always satisfactorily accommodated. The aged of Japan are likely to continue working, because of the strong work ethic, work after the age of 65 years is considered 'normal'. Thus the theory that modernization lowers the status of the aged is proved wrong in the case of Japan. Adopting a micro approach to the elderly, their problems may be viewed from the perspective of individual satisfaction. Some scientists have suggested two kinds of theories to view individual cases — the Activity Theory and Disengagement Theory. Activity theory is concerned with the extent to which the old continue their activities of middle age. Disengagement theory can be seen as the opposite of activity theory concerned as it is with the reasons and consequences of disengagement.

Sociology of Aging

Old age has in fact been important area of sociological research that a whole new field of specialization called Gerontology has come into existence. Gerontology includes in its scope many aspects (viz. biological, psychological, economic and social) of the aging process. Of these the first is taken care of by Medical Gerontology, the second by Psychology, third and fourth being an area which belongs to the realm of Sociology and Social work.

The theory of age stratification outlined by Riley Johnson and Aune Fonner considers age as a centrally important characteristic like class, sex or ethnicity, influencing individual behaviour and social structure. The theory assumes that age located individuals or groups of people are in the social structure. Each age stratum is composed of people similar in life stage who tend to share capacities, abilities and motivations to age. Age is thus a basis for structured social inequality. There is interdependence—continuing interplay between aging and social change. This interdependence is inevitable since society and individuals are inseparable. The aging process among the senior citizens of today should not be viewed as of biological and medical concern alone but of social, economic, psychological and demographical importance as well in a coordinated manner, which is the main concern of the sociological perspective approach. Further financial problem seems to be urgent, but the social psychological adjustments also need to be looked into. The problems of the old are steadily increasing in their magnitude and are generally the outcome of physical, social, economic, cultural and psychological factors, hence the right approach to handle the aging problems is coordinated, integrated and a comprehensive base which is the unique feature of the sociological perspective approach to the aging problems in the present study.

Aging is an index of deteriorating health. It may be fast or slow depending on the state of social and physical health of the citizen. It becomes a problem in respect of certain senior citizens if it becomes fast. The reasons for slow and fast aging relate closely to the social scenario.

Sociological Perspective of Aging : The Main Thrust of the Present Study

Durkheim's concept of the *Unison with the social bond* furnishes the sociological perspective for the study of aging problem among the different categories of senior citizens. This sociological perspective, being comprehensive in nature combining gerontological, social, psychological, economic and cultural factors, can well explain the aging problems of the senior citizens.

According to Durkheim's view point so long people of any class, age, gender and creed are closely knitted with social bond, they are hale and hearty and feel lesser the pinch of aging in the case of senior citizens. The moment the senior citizens feel socially isolated and disintegrated from the social bond, they begin to experience fast aging which becomes a problem.

The retired persons experience fast aging if they are deprived of the continuity to work. The senior citizens who remain actively involved in social interaction even after their retirement do not experience fast aging problems.

One of the important base of social bond in every society is religion. Those who have been all-through religious minded and maintain this tendency even after 60 years of age or retirement do not feel the problems of fast aging.

Further, those who emotionally feel the loss of social status and prestige or feel socially isolated and economically insecured after retirement or 60 years of age, they experience fast aging problems.

These are some of the sociological variables which have been validated in the present study. The comprehensiveness and holistic view point of the sociological approach has been the main attraction for the researcher. There are number of other perspectives too which could be taken advantage of in a study like this. The studies on Aging, conducted in the West, generally emphasize the psychological aspect. Some studies emphasize the economic dimension of the problem. It is assumed that economic and financial help to the retired aged persons shall be the panacea for all their problems. Hence they suggest adequate old age pension and establishment of Old Age Homes. This is a very limited approach towards the problems of the senior citizens. In short the existing studies lack comprehensive understanding of the problems of aging among the senior citizens in our country,

However, the sociological perspective approach proposed to be followed in the present study will not underrate the economic and psychological approaches. The multifacet aspects having their close relevance with the problems of aging need to be looked together in this sociological perspective approach. Such a comprehensive and holistic stand point of sociological perspective has its own significance and hence highly needed for the present study on aging among the senior citizens. Another significant feature of this sociological perspective approach is that it shall complement other studies on aging so far conducted in our country.

Global Scenario of Aging Problems

The problems of aging have drawn the attention of national and international organizations only in the last three to four decades. Though from the sixteenth century several European authors have in their publications made systematic thinking about the patterns, process and meaning of aging (Gerontology) and also made efforts to ameliorate, control and prevent the various problems of the aged.

The aging effects from industrilization and its accompaniments are of two kinds: Intrinsic and Reactive. Intrinsic effects are due to biological changes with aging. Reactive effects arise from social structures including family structure which itself is the result of industrialization and other social forces. Most old age behaviour is reactive in the sense that it is shaped by social scenario. For instance modernization affects the whole lifecycle, with changes in longevity, health standards, medication, age at marriage, age at retirement, economic circumstances and social security etc. and these affect the attitudes of the elderly.

Burgess pointed out that the modern industrial society has shifted the responsibility for the elderly away from the family. The full force of this shift has fallen heaviest on the older persons. The old in the modern age can no longer as a matter of right expect the moral and legal obligation of economic support to be provided by his children. He is less and less likely, to be offered home by a son or daughter, if ill, particularly with a chronic ailment. His children are more and more disposed to shift his care to hospital rather than provide a bed in his home. He must, more and more, look elsewhere than to descendants to provide companionship and sociability. In short, he must seek elsewhere than kins for the satisfaction of his need, both financial and health. In the west he turns to the government or to other organisations while the nature of family relationship has changed in many ways because of modernization and industrilization, the family is still a major source of primary relationship providing long lasting intimate emotional ties with others. The extent to which older people are embedded in a system of family relationship providing long lasting intimate emotional ties with others, has a great potential impact on the aging experience. We also find that the continued residence in the family home, may facilitate association with children, grandchildren, relatives, and friends which would contribute better social adjustment.

Indian Perspective on Aging Problems

With the advent of industrialization there has been a significant change in the family system. Joint families disintegrated and small nuclear families emerged where the young couple find no time to look after their old parents. In such families the position of the old has become a crucial factor. The old themselves find it difficult to adjust with the modern ways of living of their young children. In such a situation how the old in the urban set up are being looked after by the family is worth enquiring. In the cities where there is growth of individualism and with it the desire to be self-reliant. The clashes between generations, distress the old in the cities. Hence, many of the problems facing the urban elderly do not exist in the villages. In contrast to the rural population the city elderly population is quite different. Many from this group have taken recourse to Old Age Homes. Along with the lonely, the helplessness they have differences with their kith and kin perhaps the next generation, which force them to leave their own home and enter thê premises of Old Age Homes. They enjoy relatively a contented life in these Homes though they often remember earlier life as 'Golden' past. Their new life in the public environment is no doubt problem free as far as inter-relationship with family members are concerned, but after all it is an institutional life—certainly artificial being uprooted from one's familiar surroundings and implanted in a strange atmosphere which one has to accept and remain contented with. Recently in India, technological developments have caused tremendous changes in the lifestyles and values of the younger generation. Their respect for and dependence on the old is reduced. Housing shortage has made the pressure of city life unbearable for the young and even more so far the housebound old, who find their peace of mind threatened. Despite the cramped existence, the old feel lonely and deserted. They feel guilty about being old and housebound. The increase in the employment of women outside the home means their help and presence is lost to the aged in the household. Poor health, economic dependence and inability to work, lead to a loss of self-esteem. The elderly lose everything including friends, spouses, jobs, status, power, influence, income and health, none of which can be replaced. Thus they become short tempered, rigid in their attitudes, selfish and suspicious. Adjustment in the family or society becomes painful. This happens particularly when they come into conflict with the young who are exposed to an urban life style and it leads to isolation.

Finally, new standards of behaviour, new ways of spending time and money and the like provide specific grounds for conflict between the generations. The disagreements which would have remained suppressed in the past are now openly expressed. Unless the older generation remains silent, suppressing its feelings of disapproval before the young, it risks to verbal argument and contradictions, within their cultural framework, this constitutes the antithesis of appropriate modes of intergenerational communication.

In all the above ways, families which include older people are affected to the social transition taking place in an urban set up. The impact of changes on the economic structure, geographical mobility, educational and cultural values, is felt at all economic and social levels.

Aging is also a social problem because of the lag in adapting social institutions to the needs of older people without disrupting the machinery of the whole society. The problem lies in the dislocations occurring in the society because it is not prepared for having a large number of the aged. In this way in India the old face a variety of aging problems for instance the feeling of loss of social status in the family and professional status at work place, mental torture of the elderly people for being ignored, neglected, and misbehaved by their own kith and kins, intergenerational value conflict, feeling unwanted and useless creature on earth, feeling of isolation, frustrations and tensions of different sorts, feeling insecurity of all sorts etc. These aging problems are both the causes and consequences of personality, family and social disorganisation and anomie too.

Socio-Demographic View of the Elderly in India

In the beginning of the century life expectancy in India was nominal in the twenties due to all sorts of diseases and epidemics. But over the years certainly after 1947 with the triumph of medicine and growth of the health sector, life-expectancy has rapidly increased. The high rate of growth of the aged population is accounted mainly by reduction in death rate. During the period from 1901-1981, the aged population has increased by 2.58 per cent over 80 lakhs of aged people live in some 200 cities, while about 3 crores live in our villages.

Table 1.1 : Growth Rates of Total Population and of 60+ Population in India from 1951-1991

Period	*Percentage increase in total population*	*Per cent increase in 60+ population*
1951-61	24.51	22.40
1961-71	24.80	32.40
1971-81	24.75	31.60
1981-91	23.50	38.02

1911 Census series: Provisional Population totals.
Source : Govt. of India (1988).

This is a cause for concern since the population of the elderly is increased at a much faster rate than the total population as seen from the table. In the decade 1981-1991 for instance the percentage increase in the total population was approximately 23.5 while that of the 60+ was 38.02. As seen from Table 1.2 number of persons aged 60+ and their percentages are both increasing steadily.

Table 1.2 : Size and Proportion of Population of India in 60+ Age group in Census Year 1951-2001

	1951	*1961*	*1971*	*1981*	*1991*	*2001*
No. of persons (millions)	21	25	33	42	55	76
Percentage of Total Population	5.7	5.7	6.1	6.5	6.6	7.7

Note : 1991 & 2001 figures are estimated.
Source : Govt. of India 1988.

The Maharashtra Department of Social Welfare treats 60 years and above as the old age for men and 55 years for women, but such a flexible definition is very inconvenient for purposes of data analysis. Hence our definition of the old in the present study is 60 years and above for both men and women.

Table 1.3 : Percentage of the Aged Males & Females in Different Countries in 1980

	Aged 60-69		*Aged 70-79*		*Aged 80 years*	
	Male	*Female*	*Male*	*Female*	*Male*	*Female*
Australia	44.8	55.2	38.4	61.6	32.7	67.3
Egypt	46.3	53.7	44.3	55.7	41.7	58.3
France	40.7	59.3	32.8	67.2	28.6	71.4
India	51.7	48.3	51.1	48.9	49.9	50.1
Japan	43.0	57.0	41.9	58.1	37.2	62.8
Nigeria	45.2	54.8	43.7	56.3	40.6	59.4
United Kingdom	41.8	58.2	33.9	66.1	28.3	71.7
U.S.A.	42.8	57.2	36.7	63.3	33.4	66.6
World	43.9	56.1	41.6	58.4	37.1	62.9

Source : Provisional Projections of the United Nations. Population Division, New York (1979-80).

Table 1.3 clearly indicates India's top position in respect of percentage of aged males in 1980 at the global level in different old age groups, e.g. 60-69 years, 70-79 years and 80 years and above as 51.7, 51.1 and 49.9 per cent respectively in comparison to the world's position as 43.9, 41.6 and 37.1 per cent respectively.

Table 1.4 : The Expected Longevity for man and women in various Census Years After 60, 65 and 70 years of age.

Census Year	*60 +*		*65 +*		*70 +*	
	Male	*Female*	*Male*	*Female*	*Male*	*Female*
1901-11	9.0	9.3	7.3	7.6	5.8	6.0
1911-21	9.0	9.5	7.3	7.7	5.8	6.0
1921-31	9.3	9.9	7.5	8.0	6.0	6.4
1931-41	10.0	10.6	8.0	8.6	6.3	6.8
1941-51	10.0	11.4	8.8	9.2	6.8	7.3
1951-61	12.3	12.8	9.8	10.2	7.6	8.0
1961-71	14.0	14.4	11.1	11.5	8.6	8.9
1971-81	16.1	16.1	12.8	13.0	9.7	9.9
1981-91	17.3	18.0	13.7	14.5	10.4	11.0
1991-2001	18.3	20.0	14.6	15.9	11.0	12.1

Source : Malaker and Roy and Demographic Research Unit, India Statistical Institute, 1986.

As regards aging in the above table we find the expected longevity amongst males and females aged 60+ years, and 70+ years, by the end of the present century (upto 2001) in India is 18.3, 20.0, 14.6, 15.0, 11.0 and 12.1 per cent respectively.

Table 1.5 : Percentage Increase of the aged (65 years and over) for selected Asian countries and areas during 1980-2000

Country	*65+*
World	2.3
More developed region	1.3
Less developed region	3.2
Afghanistan	2.8
Burma	2.5
Bangladesh	1.6
China	3.1
India	3.8
Indonesia	3.1
Japan	3.0
Malyasia	3.1
Pakistan	2.7
Philippines	4.1
Sri Lanka	3.6

Source : Rogers (In United Nations, 1985).

As regards the position of India in Asian Countries during 1980-2000 in respect of increase in percentage of old persons of

65 years and above we find Philippines on the top as 4.1 per cent and India's neat position as 3.8 per cent.

Major Needs of the Elderly in India

There are three major needs of the elderly, viz. health needs, economic needs and socio-psychological needs. As for health needs the government alone cannot meet the needs although we have one of the best laid out medical system in the world. For an elderly person belonging to lower strata of society who lives far away from the hospital, an illness be a major calamity. If he falls ill, he cannot go to the hospital alone, he has to be accompanied by a family member who expresses his inability being a daily wage earner. Usually the family members do not care for the treatment of the elderly parents.

The main problem is lack of resources, infrastructure, will and a sound health delivery mechanism. *It can be argued that if we can have Pediatrics for treatment of children, why not have Geriatrics for treatment of the elderly?* Unfortunately there is not a single Medical School in this country where Geriatrics is taught at the under-graduate or the post-graduate level. There is one institution in Chennai where they have recently started a course on 'Geriatrics'. There are only two doctors doing this course per year. If we want to have a Geriatric hospital in every district, just imagine how many decades it will take to achieve this objective.

As for the economic aspects, there is a widespread disparity between the haves and the have-nots. In this respect both the Central and State governments have granted Old Age pensions and many other concessional facilities to the senior citizens. Although these measures have their own significance but not adequate.

In India there are 70 million elderly today, nearly 90 per cent of them are from the unorganised sector who after the age of 60 do not get any pension or gratuity or provident fund etc. and are, therefore, not linked with any medical scheme. This means that they have to continue working even after 60+. The educated can still find an alternative job or some other means of sustenance. Besides, about 40 per cent of these 70 million elderly live below the poverty line. They are mainly farm labourers, etc. When they become old their bodies cannot do the same activity as before. But they have no option but to survive. They have to continue doing these activities. About 80 per cent of these people are illiterate. And an illiterate person can do very little else, so it is not uncommon for us to see an 80 years old person pulling a rickshaw or doing some such physical activity. Out of these 70 million, half of them are women. Nearly 55 per cent of the women over the age of 60 are widows, which in our society makes them receivers rather than givers. It is a pathetic situation that elderly people who have given their best or an overwhelming majority of India's population living in rural areas especially the elderly, the situation is very bad.

The third aspect to consider is the socio-psycho and emotional needs of the aged. Following liberalization, urbanization etc. the joint family system has been broken up. There has been a significant change since independence, but the change has been particularly rapid in the three decades or so. Unfortunately, the change has been for the worse. Fifty years ago, the elderly person in Indian family unit was the Head of the family, but now the elderly have lost that privileged position. Today, in most households, the elderly person is only an appendage just another person existing. With the advent of industrialization there has been a significant change in the family system. Joint families have been disintegrated and small nuclear families have emerged where the young couple find no time to look after their old parents. Today's society is more materialistic. The elderly in such a situation have become burden on their family members and are treated as such. We bear all the time of how elderly people even in affluent families feel rejected and ignored by their family members. This was not so earlier.

The United Nations has declared 1999 as the 'International Year for older persons'. Hence let us resolve that each one of us shall look after an elderly person. If you do not have an elderly person in your family adopt one in the neighbour. Remember all of us will grow old one day.

Conclusion

India's Eighth Five Year Plan has sought to encourage voluntary or non-governmental organisations (LAGOS) to provide Old Age Homes, Day Care Centres, Mobile Medical Units and other programmes benefiting the elderly via grants on aid. To a lesser degree some State Governments have also provided resources for such programmes. The Central Government recently enacted an Old Age Assistance pension for the destitute elders similar to those already provided by all states. Further more the Central Government has been convening a small cadre of senior advocates, researchers and other experts to draft a series of objectives that shall form the basis for a National Policy on Aging. State policy makers have been invited to comment on the draft statements. In addition, State level policies specially in Maharashtra and Kerala serve as blue prints for the national efforts. Organizations created among the Indian Senior Citizens to benefit themselves and other generations are an emerging phenomenon. In 1992, the Association for senior citizens (ASC) revealed that there were approximately 125 Senior Organizations, the majority in Maharashtra. Since the other organizations have been established many of them by pensioners who now have the time, educational background and resources to devote to this kind of activity. Many are local a few such as *Help Age India* and the Federation on Aging, all are affiliated with International Organizations. These groups present monthly programmes and publish News-letter. Some have become strong advocates and have played important role in the development of State level policies for the elderly while they have yet to exercise concerted political muscle, it is anticipated in many circles that it is only a matter of time before these senior organisations become more activist, similar to senior groups in western nations.

2 RESEARCH DESIGN AND METHODOLOGY

This is a sociological study of Aging among the senior citizens based on the assumption of positive association between feeling of social alienation and fast aging. In order to make a scientific analysis of such a notion, an inevitable necessity was felt for adopting a comprehensive and holistic approach to the study of the aging problems. Hence in this study emphasis has been laid down in administering Sociological Perspective Approach considered most comprehensive and of holistic nature. Further this perspective helped in exploring reasons for the increasing ageing problems and also indicated the various ways and means of adjustment to the aging problems by the senior citizens.

OPERATIONAL DEFINITION OF THE TERMS : 'AGING', 'THE ELDERLY' OR 'THE AGED'

The 'aging' is a continued process and 'aged' is a category. The ageing as a biological phenomenon appears to begin at birth (Harrell, 1969), Ageing means the effects of age, i.e. the deterioration in physical capabilities. It is a decline in physiologic competency (Timiras, 1972) gradual decrease in adaptation to its normal environment (Strochler, 1989) etc. To Birren and Renner (1977) "aging refers to the regular changes that occur in mature genetically representative organisms as they advance in chronological age".

The 'aging of man', 'population aging' are two different concepts. The population is aged if the aged population is more than 7 per cent of the total population (U.N., 1956). The 'Aging of Population' has a simple and universally fixed accepted concept which depends upon the 'aged' people in relation to total population. Now the questions, are who are the 'aged' or the 'old' or 'Senior Citizens'.

These words have been used synonymously. The aged are those

advanced in age or the persons who live longer. According to Chamber's 20th Century Dictionary, aging is the process of growing old, on developing qualities of the old, maturing and aged organism. Thus for layman, aged is a person who has lived longer thereby suggesting a relative phenomenon.

The review of literature reveals that there are mainly three to four basic approaches which have been utilized for categorisation of the aged (Subba Rao, 1987). These approaches are physiological, psychological, socio-cultural and economic etc. There is no definite physiological, psychological or socio-cultural parameters which individually or collectively can demarcate the particular chronological age uniformly. Being a relative criteria, it will differ from species to species. The concept of 'aged' in man varies with purpose and viewpoint and also with sex, residence, climate etc. The concept will also depend upon people's viewpoint. It varies between Urban and Rural people (Biswas, 1987). Even it is conceived differently by the old and non-old. The old people look upon old age as a stage characterized by economic insecurity, poor health, loneliness and failing physiological and mental power. It is, however, useful to use a single uniform Cut-off Age for the sake of scientific study of the elderly.

Further old Age starts at different chronological age for people involved in different occupational professions. For example, people (both sexes)—in State and Central government jobs retire at 60 years of age, but few scientists in scientific organisations retire at 60 years of age. A teacher retires at 60 years of age. People in private employment generally retire after 58 years of age or later. The people in business and certain private professions retire whenever they wish (No age limit).

In summary, it is suggested that uniform Cut-off Age (say 60 years) should be adopted for the better, useable and comparable data for assessing the aging problems. Hence 60 years of Age as a Cut-off Age has been fixed in the present study for the elderly or superannuated cases among all the four categories of respondents, viz. Superannuated university teachers, Superannuated Civil Servants, Elderly lawyers and Elderly doctors under study.

Review of Researches on Aging

Indian research on the aged appeared only in the post-war era. There were occasional papers of a popular nature that highlighted the joys and woes of the evening of life. Scientific studies on the elderly in the behavioural sciences appeared in the early 1960s (Ramamurthi and Parmeshwaran, 1963, 1964). Towards the end of the decade, the *Journal of Gerontology* was launched from Jaipur with K. L. Sharma as its editor. Unfortunately the journal went out of commission a few years later only to reappear recently. Aging became an area of Doctoral research in the late 1960s and the early 1970s (Anantharaman, 1976; Pamtal, 1971 Ramamurthi, 1968; Warty, 1970). Two early research projects on the elderly were commissioned by the Planning Commission and the ICSSR (Desai and Naik, 1970; Ramamurthi, 1970). About this time, at the instance of some western experts, there was more on the part of the then government to consider the need for an Institute on Aging and a group comprising Mahalanobis, Victor D'Souza, M.S. Kanungo, P.N. Wahi and others went into the question. The Geriatric Society of India was founded in 1979 and the multi-disciplinary Association of Gerontology India (AGI) with Headquarter at B.H.U., Varanasi came into being as an affiliate to the International Association of Gerontology (IAG) in 1982. A series of seminars and conferences were organised in the area of aging by many Institutions.

Scientists and philosophers of Greece and Rome described the process of aging in terms of biological and psychological way. The Belgium Mathematician Qutelet was considered to be the first Gerontologist and he had contributed a book on the *Nature of Man and Development of his Faculties'* (1835). The first American work on Geriatrics, *Account of the State of Body and Mind in Old Age,* was published in 1973 by the physician Rush.

By 1950s, thinking and synthesizing about the problems of aging had become more significant and systematic. Landmarks in this regard were : 'The family of old people' (Peter Townsend, 1957), 'Handbook of Aging and the Individual, Psychological, Biological Aspects' (Birren, 1959), 'Handbook of Social Gerontology: Societal Aspects of Aging' (TIBBITTS, 1960) and 'Aging in Western Societies,' (Burgess, 1960). Apart from these Matild, W. Riley and her colleagues edited three Volumes : 'Ageing and Society: An Inventory of Research Findings' (Riley and Fonner 1968), 'Aging and the professions' (Riley and Johnson 1959, and 'A Sociology of Age Stratification' (Riley, Johnson and Fonner, 1972). Nevertheless, Cowdry, the author of illustrious work 'Arteriosclerosis: A summary of the problems' published in 1933 has since then, been considered as the father of modern Gerontology by many scholars. 'Becoming and being old' Sociological Approach to later life eds. Bill By the way Teresa Keil, Patrica Allatit Andaalam Brymen, 1989, 'Researching Social Gerontology : Concepts, Methods and Issues' (ed. by Sheila M. Peace, 1990). 'Aging concepts Controversies' (Second Edition Harry R. Moddy, 1990), 'Aging : An introduction to Gerontology' (Lewis R. Aiken, 1995).

With regards to developing countries like India, the studies of Gerontology are considered to be of recent development mostly by the Psychologists, Social workers, Biologists, Anthropologists and Sociologists. The pioneering works in the field of gerontology that deserve worth mentioning in this context are : ' The problems of Aged women in Batula' (Geereschiaru Kaur, 1964); 'Study of Aged in Delhi' (Ranade, 1974); 'Our elderly' (Pathak, 1980); 'Older people in Tamil Nadu' (Krishna Iyer); 'Aging and Society' (Bhatia, 1983), 'Problems of the Aged in unorganised sector' (Mahajan, 1987). In tune with the rapid growth in the field of Gerontology in India. Association of Gerontology India was founded in 1981 at BHU, Varanasi. The problems of the Aged —'A Socio-economic problems of the Aged' (S. Vijay Kumar, 1991); ' The Elderly in India' (Kumudini Dandekar, 1996); 'Psycho-Social Aspects of Aging in India' (Paramjeet Kaur Dhillon 1992); ' The problems of the old Age' (R. C. Srivastava, 1964); 'Aging-Indian Perspective and Global Scenario' (ed. Vinod Kumar, 1996); 'India's Elderly: Burden or challenge?' (S. Irudaya Rajan, U.S. Mishra, P. Sankar Sarma, 1999).

In comparison to the western countries, the studies in the field of Gerontology in India are few, for social Gerontology has evolved as a major branch of Study in India only after Independence. From the early 1980s onward the volume of Research Agencies : The DST, the ICMR, the UGC, the ICSSR and the Department of Social Welfare, Government of India considered Gerontology (Aging) as a thrust area. The International Federation on Aging (IFA) held its first Global Conference on Aging at Bombay and Pune in 1992.

Research Design

The Research design of the present study is "*Exploratory-cum-Descriptive*". This Research design needs no hypothesis testing rather exploring novel hypotheses for future researchers in the field. The fact that we had no workable hypothesis to begin with does not mean that we had no idea of the problem under study. This only means that we had no reliable adequate information about the specific reasons for increasing volume of aging problems.

Keeping the basic assumption of compatibility of aging problems and social alienation among the senior citizens in view, we did have the following hunches which were put to test and verification for the final inclusion of the findings so drawn in this study.

Tentative Hypotheses

(1) According to Drukheim's viewpoint so long people of any class age and creed are closely knitted with social bond, they are hale and hearty and feel lesser the pinch of aging. The moment the senior citizens feel socially isolated and disintegrated from the social bond, they begin to experience fast aging which becomes a problem.
(2) Following Emile Durkheim we further assume that the higher and more sudden ceasure of the elderly's social and professional involvement with concomitant loss of status and power after attaining 60 years of age or due to superannuation, the faster shall be Aging problems among the senior citizens.
(3) The deeper the religious commitment of the senior citizens the slower shall be the process of aging among the senior citizens.
(4) The higher the pinch of the loss of social status and respect in the family among the senior citizens, the more shall be the aging problems.
(5) The higher the degree of personality and family disorganization among the senior citizens, the acuter and sharper shall be the problems of aging.
(6) The larger the extent of comprehensive social security and welfare measures, the least shall be the intensity of aging problems among the senior citizens.

Determining Representative Sample Size of the Respondents

The universe of the Research is Gorakhpur city. It was so decided because of no provision of help from a Research Fellow/Associate, in the present sanctioned project for administering an *Interview Schedule* on the different categories of respondents scattered over the entire City, District, State and other States. The establishment of personal contact with the large number of respondents located in a large network was not possible by a single principal investigator alone. Hence while determining the representative sample size of about 240 respondents it was decided to include in the sample such respondents easily available and accessible within the Gorakhpur city premises. These 240 total respondents in this study are of four categories, viz. Superannuated university teachers, civil servants, elderly doctors and elderly lawyers.

In order to constitute the Representative sample size of superannuated university teacher and public servants, first of all a cut-off year was fixed for the purpose of inclusion in the sample size, cases aged more than 80 years, hence 1978 was taken as a base, i.e. a 'Cut-off year'. All the cases of superannuation of university teachers and public servants were calculated since 1978 and onward. The other considerations were the availability and easy accessibility of the respondents in Gorakhpur city.

As per official record of superannuation with the Gorakhpur University Pension Cell we found the total number, i.e. 105 superannuated university teachers since 1978. In order to constitute a Representative sample size 40 per cent cases (i.e. 42) of the total universe (i.e. 105) were randomly selected.

As regards superannuated civil servants we defined civil servant as "a Central and State Government employee of an officer cadre both Gazetted and non-gazetted and also appointed directly or 'the promotees'. There is hardly any state agency or department here in Gorakhpur, which can provide complete information about the State government superannuated public servants. On the other hand N.E. Railway Officers Pension Cell provided the complete record of its superannuated public servants. As per their record about 816 N.E. Railway Public servants were superannuated so far since 1978. The problem was that all the superannuated public servants were not locally available. Fortunately as per Railway record there were about 102 N.E. Railway superannuated public servants locally residing. Hence these 102 cases were considered the total universe and 40 per cent of this total universe, i.e. 40 in number constituted Representative sample size of civil servants for the purpose of the present study.

As per training and expertise of the lawyers in Gorakhpur district courts we can distribute them in five major wings, viz. Civil, Criminal,

Revenue, Taxation and Railway claims wings. There are about 3000 total number of lawyers in Gorakhpur district Courts broadly distributed as 1200 in Civil, 1200 in Criminal, 500 in Revenue, 60 in Taxation and 40 in Railway claims divisions. As regard the elderly lawyers, i.e. those above 60 years of age we found such cases to the extent of about 10 per cent of the total 3000 lawyers, i.e. 300 was taken as the total universe of the Elderly lawyers and 40 per cent of these cases, i.e. 120 constituted a Representative sample size. These 120 cases were selected with much difficulty through many rounds of visits to the District Courts.

As regards Elderly doctors, i.e. those of 60 years of age and above fortunately we found a list of 145 doctor members of GPO (General Practitioners Association) Gorakhpur city. The President of the Association helped me in ticking out those doctor members in the list who were 60 years of age and above. Such cases were only 28 in total number. Further we also collected information about 10 cases superannuated from the Civil Hospital, Railway Hospital and Medical College. In this way the total universe of 38 Elderly doctors being a manageable number constituted a Representative sample size of the Elderly doctors for the study.

Now the final position of the total number of representative sample size of different categories has been finalised as Superannuated university teachers 42, Superannuated civil servants 40, Elderly lawyers 120, Elderly doctors 38 and the total respondents as 240.

Research Techniques 'Interview' and 'Observation' Schedules Administered

The most appropriate research technique for the collection of reliable primary information about the problem under study is an 'Interview Schedule' . In this way an Interview Schedule was carefully prepared and pre-tested before the final launch. As a result of its pilot testing among the different categories of respondents, some of the questions appeared irrelevant, insignificant and leading ones, were dropped and many new, relevant and necessary questions were added afresh.

While framing the 'Interview Schedule' the following aspects were kept in view :

(i) The Socio-economic and cultural perspectives of the respondents.

(ii) The nature of family and social relationships of the respondents.
(iii) The extent of personality and family disorganisation among the elderly.
(iv) The physical and mental health conditions of the respondents.
(v) The extent of social distance, cohesion and segregation amongst the respondents.
(vi) Self-centred *vs* other oriented personality pattern of the respondents.
(vii) Both the distinctive and common modes of efforts on the part of senior citizens towards reconciliation, adaptation and adjustment to the various aging problems.

Besides an 'Observation Schedule' was also planned. This was so needed because of the variety of respondents under study and they may like some exclusive questions in the schedule specifically related to their background and to their profession. And this shall encourage them to expose their views, opinion and attitudes towards aging problems and the degree of their tie with the social bond of unison. Hence, instead of preparing different 'Interview Schedules' for the different categories of respondents, it was decided to plan an 'Observation Schedule' (containing exclusive questions of interest and attraction to all the different categories of respondents in respect of the causes and extent of aging problems.

In this way both 'Interview Schedule' and 'Observation Schedule' were simultaneously prepared and administered on the different categories of the respondents and thereby both common and varying information, opinion towards aging problems were gathered and valuable findings obtained.

Collection of Primary and Secondary Data

The primary data, were collected through the pre-tested and modified 'Interview Schedule' consisting of four sections A, B, C, D. In the first section 'A' there are questions concerning Respondents' 'Identification data', i.e. Family, Age group, caste, community, profession, Income before and after 60 years of age and dwelling place. The next section 'B' includes questions about socio-cultural adjustments such as family relations. Nature and frequency of responses towards the Elderly by their children and grandchildren, feeling of loneliness and social alienation, participation in family functions, relations with neighbours and friends etc. The third section 'C' concerns questions mainly relating to Economic adjustments such as: Views regarding continuity to work/job/profession; Adequacy of Income/Pension, Base of support to fall back upon in Contingency; Sources and Agencies of Economic help etc. The last section 'D' relates with the Bio-psychological aspects of the aging problems such as Geriatric problems, Aid Instruments needed and used, general health conditions; Diseases; types of treatment, Routine activities such as Meals, Appetite, sleep etc.; Faith and leaning toward spiritual and religious rites, Expectation of blessed award from God in return of ritualistic performance, Leisure time activities; Liking for Old Age Homes, Unpleasant Aspects of life; Chief Problems of Aging felt; Chief desires and Wishes and Expectations from the State and Central Governments in the form of financial relief; subsidy, concessions in Bus and Railway fares; Rationed food and priority in providing dwelling place etc.

The field data so collected were scientifically analysed to assess the different aging problems of the aged and to work out the degree of positive and negative association with the postulated Independent Variable of 'Feeling of Social Alienation' with the aging problems. The variables were divided into 'Independent' and 'Dependent' ones. In the present study although the Chief Independent variable is 'Social Alienation' but others are also such as: 'Sex', 'Age', 'Marital status', 'Income', 'family size' and 'relationships' etc. whereas main dependent variables are health, diseases, types of treatment, difficulties in daily routine life, nature of relations of the aged with the family members, changes in the attitudes of the family members towards the aged, frequency of visit to native home by the children and grand-children, the elderly's stand in taking decision in family matters and the extent of maintaining command and respect of the aged in the family, state of loneliness, irritation, proper care towards the upkeep of the elderly in the family.

Besides, the secondary information and data were also collected through National and International censuses and population projections, National Sample Survey Reports, National and International Journals on Social Gerontology, Books, Magazines, Newspapers, Articles on the Aging problems.

The principal investigator of the present study visited Central Library of the Tata Institute of Social Sciences, Mumbai and consulted the relative relevant literature for about a week. Again on visit to the Advanced Centre of Research on Aging in S.V. University, Tirupati (Chennai) for about five days the researcher consulted the very rich library of the Department of Psychology, S.V. University, Tirupati, which provided many valuable secondary information about hundreds of Psychological scales tested on the aged in different studies on aging problems among the senior citizens. The visit and stay for a day or two at B.H.U. Varanasi, Central Library also benefited much with a lot of secondary information about the aged and the aging problems in India.

Tabulation and Statistical Application

Both the primary and secondary data so collected were condensed, processed and put to the tabular analysis on multi-dimensional levels with the frequencies and their respective percentages. Then the application of the relevant statistical formulae helped in deriving comparative assessment of the aging problems among the respondents of different categories under study. In this way the results so obtained and interpreted, were the major sources of valuable findings of the present study.

Difficulties Felt and Rapport Established

Initially the researcher had to face the cold responses from the respondents of two categories, viz. the Elderly Doctors and the Elderly Lawyers. It was so because of much of the preoccupations in their professions. Hence the investigator visited their residences many times at their appointed leisure time to help them in filling up the Interview Schedule supplied to them personally.

On the whole many efforts were made to establish a close rapport with the respondents by accompanying them in morning walk in the city and university parks and frequently visiting their places of residences. The principal investigator of the present study being himself a superannuated university teacher became life member of the Senior Citizens Forum, Gorakhpur. This offered me (the Principal Investigator) a good opportunity of meeting closely with the senior citizen available in the city.

As a result of all these efforts although in the beginning there was not a good response from the respondents of certain categories but later on after convincing them the utility and purpose of the present study and explaining them some of the questions of the Interview Schedule personally by visiting their places, we ultimately could gain their confidence and then found quick, prompt and intimate response from the respondents of all the categories towards answering questions pertaining to both the 'Interview and Observation' Schedules and thereby we obtained valuable information in the right earnest way about the extent of Association between different aging problems and the extent of the feeling of Social Alienation among the senior citizens. In this way the main thrust of the present study, *i.e.* Sociological perspective approach has chiefly been worked out in the present study.

Dimensions of the Present Study

After discussing the Sociological perspective of the aging problem at the global level and in Indian Context under Chapter-I, we tried to select an appropriate Research design and Methodology in Chapter-II. In this respect after formulating the tentative hypotheses for the present study and determining the sample size of the respondents, the relative research techniques, viz. Interview and Observation Schedules were finalized in such a way that we may be able to collect all the relevant information from the different categories of respondents through the administration of a single Interview Schedule. In Chapter-III on Socio-Economic Profile of the respondents we pinpointed in locating the position of the respondents in Age and family group, caste, community, profession and income group, present and past sources of income and securities and their Inter-Intra social relationships in the society. In Chapter-IV we explored the ways and means of socio-cultural adjustments to the aging problems on the part of all the respondents. Then we tried to find out the emergent economic status of the respondents due to aging process and their capacity to cope with aging problems in Chapter-V. The Bio-Psychological aging problems such as stresses, strains, feeling of loneliness, social alienation, their suppressed desires and emotions, health condition, Diseases, Treatment, and Leisure Time activities etc. were discovered and modes of reconciliation with them to what extent on the part of the different categories of the respondents in Chapter-VI. Lastly in Chapter-VII on 'In Lieu of Conclusion', major findings, discussion and various suggestions were detailed out and also a highlight on National Policy for the Aged in India.

3 SOCIO-ECONOMIC PROFILE OF THE RESPONDENTS

Introduction

The sample size of the present study is 240 senior citizens of different professions such as teaching, administration, legal and medical respectively distributed as 42 superannuated University teachers, 40 superannuated civil servants, 120 elderly lawyers and 38 elderly doctor's of Gorakhpur region. Hence there shall be diversities in the social economic profile of the respondents under study. The two categories of respondents, viz. University teachers and civil servants are senior citizens by virtue of their superannuation in their services generally after 60 years of age, while the other two categories of respondents are private practitioners, elderly lawyers and doctors. They do not have any mandatory retirement or superannuated age. In the present study for these respondents a cutout age of 60 years was fixed for considering them an Elderly, hence they were treated as senior citizens and addressed as Elderly Lawyers and Elderly Doctors if they have crossed 60 years of age.

In the socio-economic profile of all the respondents we have tried to locate their position in the age, gender, marital, status, caste, community, profession and income groups. The nature of their dwelling place, family and economic background as well as their views about disengagement from work or retaining continuity of work even after 60 years of age etc. were probed into. Hence in this analysis of socio-economic profile of the respondents we shall find the variety of facets and views etc. about Aging and its relative problems among the senior citizens.

Community and the Age Groups of the Respondents

The senior citizens of different age groups and communities are distributed as 208, 18, 08 and 06 respectively for Hindus, Muslims, Christians and Sikhs. Table 3.1 further shows the distribution of each community among the different categories of respondents, viz. 42 superannuated university teachers, 40 civil servants, 120 elderly lawyers and 38 doctors.

The distribution of Hindu respondents is as 39, 35, 102, and 32; Muslim respondents as 1, 2, 11 and 4; Christian respondents as 1, 3, 3 and 1; Sikh respondents as 1, nil, 4 and 1 respectively among the superannuated university teachers, civil servants, elderly lawyers and doctors.

Among the superannuated university teachers the community-wise distribution in the age group of 60-70 years is as 20, 1, 1 and 1 respectively among the Hindus, Muslims, Christians and Sikhs; in other age groups such as 71-80 years and 81 years and above there are only Hindu respondents in both the above age groups to the extent of 18 and 1 respectively.

Among the superannuated civil servants the community-wise distribution of the respondents in different age groups is as 20, 2, and 2 respectively among the Hindu, Muslim and Christian respondents in 60-70 years of age; in another age group of 71-80 years of age there are 15 Hindus and 1 Christian and none in the last age group of 81 years and above age group.

Among the elderly lawyers we find community-wise distribution of respondents in different age groups is as 70, 8, 2, and 3 respectively for the Hindus, Muslims, Christians and Sikhs in the age group of 60-70 years; as 25, 3, 1 and 1 respectively among Hindus, Muslims, Christians and Sikhs in the age group of 71-80 years; and only 7 Hindus in the last age group of 81 years and above.

Among the elderly doctors we find distribution as 12, 2 and 1 respectively for Hindus, Muslims and Christians in the age group of 60-70 years and as 18, 2 and 1 respectively for Hindus, Muslims and Christians in the age group of 60-70 years and as 18, 2 and 1 respectively for Hindus, Muslims and Sikhs in the next age group of 71-80 years and only 2 Hindus in the last age group of 81 years and above.

The above analysis shows two major facts, viz. the dominant age group as 60-70 years (60%) and the dominant community as Hindus (87%) among all the four categories of respondents.

Table 3.1 : Community and Age Groups

	Superannuated Univ. teachers							
	Age Group							
	60-70 yrs		*71-80 yrs*		*81 yrs & above*		*Total*	
	f	%	f	%	f	%	f	%
Hindu	20	88	18	100	01	100	39	94
Muslim	01	04	–	–	–	–	01	02
Christian	01	04	–	–	–	–	01	02
Sikh	01	04	–	–	–	–	01	02
Total	23	100	18	100	01	100	42	100

	Superannuated Civil Servants							
	Age Group							
	60-70 yrs		*71-80 yrs*		*81 yrs & above*		*Total*	
	f	%	f	%	f	%	f	%
Hindu	20	84	15	94	–	–	35	87
Muslim	02	08	–	–	–	–	02	05
Christian	02	08	01	06	–	–	03	08
Sikh	–	–	–	–	–	–	–	–
Total	24	100	16	100	–	–	40	100

	Elderiy Lawyers							
	Age Group							
	60-70 yrs		*71-80 yrs*		*81 yrs & above*		*Total*	
	f	%	f	%	f	%	f	%
Hindu	70	84	25	84	07	100	102	86
Muslim	08	10	03	10	–	–	11	09
Christian	02	02	01	03	–	–	03	02
Sikh	03	04	01	03	–	–	04	03
Total	83	100	30	100	07	100	120	100

	Elderiy Doctors							
	Age Group							
	60-70 yrs		*71-80 yrs*		*81 yrs & above*		*Total*	
	f	%	f	%	f	%	f	%
Hindu	12	80	18	86	02	–	32	84
Muslim	02	13	02	09	–	–	04	10
Christian	01	07	–	–	–	–	01	03
Sikh	–	–	01	05	–	–	01	03
Total	15	100	21	100	02	100	38	100

Caste and Age group

As regards caste and age group we have analysed the three levels of caste, viz. Higher, Middle and Lower among the total of 208 Hindu respondents. They are distributed as 39, 35, 102 and 32 respectively among the superannuated university teachers, civil servants, elderly lawyers and doctors.

In Table 3. 2 we find distribution of Hindu respondents among the superannuated university teachers as 22 and 17 respectively for higher and middle levels of castes; among the superannuated civil servants as 21 and 14 respectively for higher and middle levels; among the elderly lawyers as 48, 43 and 11 respectively for higher, middle and lower levels of castes and among the elderly doctors as 22 and 10 respectively for higher and middle castes.

Among the superannuated university teachers higher caste respondents are as 12, 8 and 02 and middle caste respondents as 8, 8 and 1 respectively in the age groups of 60-70 years, 71-80 years and 81 vears and above.

Among the superannuated civil servants higher caste respondents are as 12, 8 and 1 and middle caste respondents as 6, 6, and 2 respectively in the age groups of 60-70 years, 71-80 years and 81 years and above.

Among the elderly lawyers higher caste respondents are as 30, 15 and 3; middle caste respondents as 30, 10, and 3; and lower caste respondents as 5, 4, and 2 respectively in the age groups of 60-70 years, 71-80 years and 81 years and above.

Among the elderly doctors higher caste respondents are as 15, 6 and 1 and middle caste respondents as 5, 5 and nil respectively in the age groups of 60-70 years, 71-80 years and 81 years and above.

Job/Profession

Profession/Job Before and After Superannuation/60 years of Age

Although the respondents under study are from different professions like teaching, administration, legal and medical but after becoming senior citizens (i.e. after superannuation or attaining 60 years of age) we find change in the form of discontinuity and complete abandonment of profession and job they were undertaking before.

Table 3.3 gives an account of all these happenings with the

Table 3.2 : Castes and the Age Groups

	Saperannuated Univ. Teachers								*Superannuated Civil Servants*								*Elderly Lawyers*								*Elderiy Doctors*							
	Caste								*Caste*								*Caste*								*Caste*							
	Higher		*Middle*		*Lower*		*Total*		*Higher*		*Middle*		*Lower*		*Total*		*Higher*		*Middle*		*Lower*		*Total*		*Higher*		*Middle*		*Lower*		*Total*	
	f	%	f	%	f	%	f	%	f	%	f	%	f	%	f	%	f	%	f	%	f	%	f	%	f	%	f	%	f	%	f	%
60–70 yrs	12	55	8	47	–	–	20	51	12	57	06	43	–	–	18	51	30	63	30	70	5	46	65	64	15	68	5	50	–	–	26	63
71–80 yrs	08	36	8	47	–	–	16	41	08	38	06	43	–	–	14	40	15	31	10	23	4	36	29	28	06	27	5	50	–	–	11	34
81 yrs & above	02	09	01	06	–	–	03	8	01	05	02	14	–	–	03	09	03	06	03	07	2	18	08	08	01	05	–	–	–	–	01	03
Total	22	100	17	100	–	–	39	100	21	100	14	100	–	–	35	100	48	100	43	100	11	100	102	100	22	100	10	100	–	–	32	100

Table 3.3 : Continuity of Job/Profession

Continuity of Job/Profession	*Superannuated university teachers*		*Superannuated Civil Servant*		*Elderly Lawyers*		*Elderly Doctors*		*Total*	
	f	*%*	*f*	*%*	*f*	*%*	*f*	*%*	*f*	*%*
Continuing The Same Job/ Profession as Before	–	–	–	–	118	98	38	100	156	65
Shifted To Other Job/ Profession	07	17	10	25	02	02	–	–	19	08
Discontinued & Doing/ No Job Profession	35	83	30	75	–	–	–	–	65	27
Total	42	100	40	100	120	100	38	100	240	100

professions/jobs of the respondents. The elderly lawyers and doctors generally continue their profession even after attaining 60 years of age. Even some of the elderly lawyers and doctors once 'Government servant preferred continuation of their respective profession after superannuation. The incidents of change, discontinuity of job/ profession and doing nothing after superannuation are common among the retired teachers and civil servants. The shift to other profession/ job and continuity of work appear to the extent of 17 and 25 per cent respectively among the superannuated teachers and civil servants. On the other hand the cases of doing nothing are also found among the superannuated teachers and civil servants to the extent of 83 and 75 per cent respectively. This shows no job or work for them.

Economic Status

Table 3.4 records the rise and fall in the economic status on the basis of income groups of the respondents were before/after the superannuation or 60 years of age. In this regard there is a fall in the economic level among both the superannuated university teachers and civil servants as before superannuation, the university teachers were in the higher income groups of Rs. 5 to Rs. 8 thousand p.m., Rs. 8 to Rs. 15 thousand p.m. and Rs. 15 to Rs. 25 thousand p.m. to the extent of 5, 35 and 60 per cent respectively, are now distributed to the extent of 60, 24 and 16 per cent in the income groups of upto Rs. 3 thousand p.m., Rs. 3 to Rs. 5 thousand p.m., and Rs. 5 to Rs. 8 thousand p.m.,

Table 3.4 : Income Groups of the Respondents Before and After Superannuation or 60 years of Age

Income group in thousand p.m.	*Superannuated university teachers*				*Superannuated public servants*				*Elderly Lawyers*				*Elderly Doctors*			
	Before 60 yrs		*After 60 yrs*		*Before 60 yrs*		*After 60 yrs*		*Before 60 yrs*		*After 60 yrs*		*Before 60 yrs*		*After 60 yrs*	
	f	*%*	*f*	*%*	*f*	*%*	*f*	*%*	*f*	*%*	*f*	*%*	*f*	*%*	*f*	*%*
Upto Rs. 3 p.m.	–	–	25	60	–	–	–	–	73	61	80	67	–	–	–	–
Above Rs. 3 upto Rs. 5 p.m.	–	–	10	24	–	–	15	38	17	14	20	17	–	–	–	–
Above Rs. 5 upto Rs. 8 p.m.	02	05	07	16	15	38	25	62	10	08	07	06	–	–	–	–
Above Rs. 8 to Rs. 15 p.m.	15	35	–	–	20	50	–	–	12	10	07	06	–	–	–	–
Above Rs. 15 upto Rs. 25 p.m.	25	60	–	–	05	12	–	–	08	07	06	04	–	–	–	–
Above Rs. 25 upto Rs. 35 p.m.	–	–	–	–	–	–	–	–	–	–	–	–	25	66	–	–
Above Rs. 35 upto Rs. 45 p.m.	–	–	–	–	–	–	–	–	–	–	–	–	10	26	–	–
Above Rs. 45 upto Rs. 55 p.m.	–	–	–	–	–	–	–	–	–	–	–	–	03	08	03	08
Above Rs. 55 upto Rs. 65 p.m.	–	–	–	–	–	–	–	–	–	–	–	–	–	–	15	39
Above Rs. 65 upto Rs. 75 p.m.	–	–	–	–	–	–	–	–	–	–	–	–	–	–	20	53
Above Rs. 75 p.m. & onward	–	–	–	–	–	–	–	–	–	–	–	–	–	–	–	
Total	42	100	42	100	40	100	100	100	120	100	120	100	38	100	38	100

respectively. In respect of superannuated civil servants we find the same trend of fall in the economic status after superannuation. The distribution of the respondents of civil servants before superannuation was in the higher income groups of Rs. 5 to Rs. 8 thousand p.m., Rs. 8 to Rs. 15 thousand p.m. and Rs. 15 to Rs. 25 thousand p.m. to the extent of 38, 50 and 12 per cent respectively, are now in the lower income groups to the extent of 38 and 62 per cent in Rs. 3 to Rs. 5 thousand p.m. and Rs. 5 to Rs. 8 thousand p.m. respectively.

The distribution of the elderly lawyers before 60 years of age in different income groups was to the extent of 61, 14, 08, 10 and 07 per cent respectively in the income groups as upto Rs. 3 thousand p.m., Rs. 3 to Rs. 5 thousand p.m.; Rs. 5 to Rs. 8 thousand p.m., Rs. 8 to Rs. 15 thousand p.m. and Rs. 15 to 25 thousand p.m. have now shifted toward higher income groups after 60 years of age to the extent of 41, 21, 21, 10 and 07 per cent respectively in the income groups as upto Rs. 3 thousand p.m., Rs. 3 to Rs. 5 thousand p.m., Rs. 5 to Rs. 8 thousand p.m., and Rs. 8 to Rs. 15 thousand p.m. Similar is the case with the elderly doctors after 60 years of age. We find their distribution before 60 years of age to the extent of 66, 26 and 08 per cent relating to the income groups of Rs. 25 to Rs. 35 thousand p.m., Rs. 35 to Rs. 45 thousand p.m. and Rs. 45 to Rs. 55 thousand p.m. has now climbed up to the extent of 08, 39 and 53 per cent in the higher income groups after 60 years of age as Rs. 45 to Rs. 55 thousand p.m., Rs. 55 to Rs. 65 thousand p.m. and Rs. 65 to Rs. 75 thousand p.m. respectively.

Sources of Income Before and After Superannuation or 60 Years of Age

Some changes and additions have been reported in the sources of income before and after superannuation or 60 years of age among all the different categories of respondents in Table 3.5. The major change in the sources of income among the superannuated university teachers and civil servants is from salary to pension. Besides some new sources of income after superannuation among the university teachers are : Honorarium (48%), Interest on Fixed Deposit (24%), Tuition, coaching and counselling (10%), Royalty on Books and Guides (14%), Income from sale of agricultural produce (7%). In respect of civil servants after superannuation the new sources of income besides pension are : Interest on Fixed deposit (25%), and rent from Houses, land and shops

Table 3.5 : Sources of Income Before and After 60 years of Age or Superannuation

Sources	*Superannuated university teachers*				*Superannuated public servants*				*Elderly Lawyers*				*Elderly Doctors*			
	Before 60 yrs		*After 60 yrs*		*Before 60 yrs*		*After 60 yrs*		*Before 60 yrs*		*After 60 yrs*		*Before 60 yrs*		*After 60 yrs*	
	f	%	*f*	%	*f*	%	*f*	%	*f*	%	*f*	%	*f*	%	*f*	%
Pension	–	–	42	100	–	–	40	100	–	–	–	–	–	–	04	11
Honorarium	–	–	20	48	–	–	–	–	–	–	–	–	–	–	–	–
Salary	42	100	–	–	40	100	–	–	–	–	–	–	04	11	–	–
Consultation Fee	–	–	–	–	–	–	–	–	–	–	–	–	34	89	38	100
Lawyers' Fee	–	–	–	–	–	–	–	–	120	100	120	100	–	–	–	–
Interest on Fixed Deposits	02	04	10	24	02	05	10	25	14	12	40	33	25	66	38	100
Tuition, Coaching & Guiding	–	–	04	10	–	–	–	–	–	–	–	–	–	–	–	–
Royalty on Books & Guides	02	05	06	14	–	–	–	–	–	–	–	–	–	–	–	–
Rent from Shops & Houses & Land	–	–	–	–	02	05	05	12	10	08	20	17	10	26	25	66
Income from sale of Agricultural Produce	03	07	03	07	–	–	–	–	60	50	70	58	05	13	10	26
Running Auto, Taxi, Rickshaw/ Tractor/Truck/Bus etc.	–	–	–	–	–	–	–	–	10	08	35	29	–	–	–	–
Earning from Clinics and Establishments	–	–	–	–	–	–	–	–	–	–	10	08	05	13	15	39

etc. (12%). As regards the elderly lawyers, after 60 years of age besides lawyers Fee, other new sources of income are : interest on Fixed Deposit 33 per cent, Rent from House and land and shops etc. (17%), Income from sale of agricultural produce (58%), Income from running Auto, taxi, Rickshaws, Truck and bus etc. (29%) and income from new establishment (8%). In respect of elderly doctors besides their consultation fee and pension to about four doctors previously served in Government hospitals, the other sources of income after 60 years of age are : Interest on Fixed deposit by all the 38 doctors, Rent from Houses, shops and land (66%), Income from sale of agricultural produce (26%) and eaming from private clinics (39%).

On the whole there are good number of novel additions in the sources of income with increased volume are found with the elderly doctors and not so much in the case of elderly lawyers. On the other hand there are additions of only few new resources of income with the university teachers and civil servants after superannuation.

Marital Status of the Respondents

In Table 3.6 we find 20 (08%) female senior citizens among all the four categories of respondents, distributed as 3 (7%), 4 (10%), 10(8%), and 3 (8%) respectively among the superannuated university teachers, civil servants, elderly lawyers and doctors.

As regards marital status of all the respondents we find married 201 (84%). widow/widower 22(09%) and divorced 17 (7%).

The categorywise distribution of respondents is: as 88, 05 and 07 per cent, respectively for married, widow/widower and divorced among the superannuated university teachers, as 80, 10, 10 per cent respectively for married, widow/widower and divorced among the superannuated Civil servants; as 83, 10, and 07 per cent respectively for married, widow/widower and divorced among the elderly lawyers and similarly as 87, 10 and 03 per cent respectively for married, widow/widower and divorced among the elderly doctors.

The two clear facts about the respondents on the whole are majority of them are male (92%) and married (84%).

Type of Family

Every respondent is a member of a particular family. In Indian context there are three major types of family at present, viz. Joint, Nuclear

Table 3.6 : Sex and Marital Status

Sex & Marital Status	*Superannuated university teachers*		*Superannuated Civil Servants*		*Elderly Lawyers*		*Elderly Doctors*		*Total*	
	f	*%*	*f*	*%*	*f*	*%*	*f*	*%*	*f*	*%*
Male	39	193	36	90	110	92	35	92	220	92
Female	04	07	04	10	10	08	03	08	20	08
Total	42	100	40	100	120	100	38	100	240	100
Married	37	88	32	80	99	83	33	87	201	84
Widow/ Widower	02	05	04	10	12	10	04	10	22	09
Divorced/ Separated	003	07	04	10	9	07	01	03	17	07
Total	42	100	40	100	120	100	38	100	240	100

and Extended. On the whole the families of all the 240 respondents are distributed as Joint 185 (77%), Nuclear 39 (16%), and extended 16 (7%) types of family in Table 3.7

Table 3.7 : Type of Family

Type of Family	*Superannuated university teachers*		*Superannuated Civil Servants*		*Elderly Lawyers*		*Elderly Doctors*		*Total*	
	f	*%*	*f*	*%*	*f*	*%*	*f*	*%*	*f*	*%*
Joint	30	71	35	88	90	75	30	79	185	77
Nuclear	10	24	04	10	20	17	05	13	39	16
Extended	02	05	01	02	10	08	03	08	16	07
Total	42	100	40	100	120	100	38	100	240	100

Further the family types among the categorywise respondents are distributed as: 30 (71%), 10 (24%), and 02 (5%) respectively for Joint, Nuclear and Extended types among the superannuated university teachers, as 35 (80%), 04(10%), and 01(2%) respectively for joint, nuclear and extended ones among the superannuated civil servants; as 90 (75%); 20 (17%) and 10 (8%) respectively for joint, nuclear and extended family types among the elderly lawyers, similarly as 30(79%), 05(13%), and 3(8%) respectively for Joint, Nuclear and Extended types among the elderly doctors. In spite of much migration and mobility amongst the youths in modern family, the native family type is of the joint nature (77%).

Family Lineage

The other facet of family background type of the respondents is the number of members of different generations living together in a family. Corresponding to the popular family types, viz. nuclear, extended and joint there are three types of family, i.e. one constituting members of a single generation, the other containing members of two generations and the last one having members of three generations or more together. In this respect we find distribution of family types of the respondents in Table 3.8 as 16 (7%), 39 (16%) and 185 (77%) respectively for single generation, two generation and three generation or more family types among all the 240 respondents on the whole.

Table 3.8 : Number of Generation in a Family

No. of generation in a family	*Superannuated university teachers*		*Superannuated Civil Servants*		*Elderly Lawyers*		*Elderly Doctors*		*Total*	
	f	*%*	*f*	*%*	*f*	*%*	*f*	*%*	*f*	*%*
Single	02	05	01	02	10	8	03	08	16	07
Double	10	24	04	10	20	17	05	13	39	16
Triple	30	71	35	88	90	75	30	79	185	77
Total	42	100	40	100	120	100	38	100	240	100

The distribution of number of generation-wise family types among the different categories of the respondents under study is as 02 (50%), 10 (34%) and 30 (71%) respectively for single, double land triple generation family types among the superannuated university teachers, as 01 (2%), 4 (10 %), and 35 (88%) respectively for single, double and triple generation family types among the superannuated civil servants. Further among the elderly lawyers the distribution is as 10 (8%), 20 (17%) and 90 (75%) respectively for single, double and triple generation family types and as 3 (8%), 5 (13%) and 30 (79%) respectively for single, double and triple generation family types among the elderly doctors.

The above analysis again confirms the joint family a dominant pattern among the majority of the respondents under study.

Dwelling Place

The dwelling place is a sort of shelter and a secured place to live for the senior citizens. In Table 3.9 we find that superannuated and those crossed 60 years of age are so much security minded senior citizens that most of them 163 (68%) have their own houses, only 62 (26%) live in rented houses. The rest of the elderly 8 (3%) either live in neighbour's/friend's houses or 7 (3%) put up with their relatives.

Table 3.9 : Type of Dwelling Place

Type of dwelling place	*Superannuated University Teachers*		*Superannuated Civil Servants*		*Elderly Lawyers*		*Elderly Doctors*		*Total*	
	f	*%*	*f*	*%*	*f*	*%*	*f*	*%*	*f*	*%*
Own House	30	72	15	38	82	68	36	95	163	68
Rented House	10	24	20	50	30	25	02	05	62	26
Neighbour's/ Friend's house	01	02	02	05	05	04	–	–	08	03
Relative's house	01	02	03	07	03	03	–	–	07	03
Total	42	100	40	100	120	100	38	100	240	100

The distribution of dwelling places as per category-wise respondents is as 30 (72%), 10 (21%), 01 (2%), and 1 (2%) respectively for own, rented, neighbour's /friend's and relative's house among the superannuated university teachers, as 15(38%), 20(50%), 02(5%) and 3(7%) respectively for own, rented, neighbour's/friend's and relatives house among the superannuated civil servants. Similarly among the elderly lawyers it is as 82 (68%), 30 (25%), 5 (4%) and 3 (3%) respectively for own, rented, neighbour's, friend's and relative's house and among the elderly doctors it is as 36(95%) own house and 2 (5%) live in rented houses.

Views About when and why to Retire from Active service/ work/ profession

There is no mandatory age of retirement for the private practitioner elderly lawyers and doctors. Hence their views were obtained in this respect. They were asked to suggest two cut-out ages, viz. the Age for slowing down their active involvement in their legal and medical profession (Table 3.10). Although they were not in favour of thinking cut-out ages for slowing down their active engagement and withdrawing themselves completely from their work but anyhow they

Table 3.10 : Prefering the Age for Slowing Down their active Job/Profession by Elderly Lawyers and Doctors

Preferred Age	*Elderly Lawyers*		*Elderly Doctors*		*Total*	
	f	%	*f*	%	*f*	%
50 years of age	–	–	01	03	01	0.5
58 years of age	–	–	01	03	01	0.5
60 years of age	30	25	05	13	35	22
65 years of age	25	21	04	11	29	18
70 years of age	38	32	06	15	44	28
75 years of age	01	01	05	13	06	04
80 years of age	01	01	01	03	02	01
Never	25	20	15	39	40	26
Total	120	100	38	100	158	100

were mostly in favour of 70 years as a cutout age for slowing down their professional activities to the extent of 38 (30%) and 6 (.5%) respectively for elderly lawyers and doctors' views. Further in Table 3.11 there was no consensus about the cutout age for completely ceasure of their professional work. They suggested different cutout ages for complete retirement as 70 years of age by the elderly lawyers (33%) and 80 years of age by the elderly doctors (39%). Further the equal number and percentage i.e. 15 (39%) among the elderly lawyers and doctors say Never retirement from their profession.

Table 3.11 : Proposed Age for Complete Retirement from Active Profession/Job by Elderly Lawyers & Doctors

Proposed Age	*Elderly Lawyers*		*Elderly Doctors*		*Total*	
	f	%	*f*	%	*f*	%
65 years of age	30	25	–	–	30	19
70 years of age	40	33	03	09	43	27
75 years of age	20	17	05	13	25	15
80 years of age	05	04	15	39	20	13
Never	25	21	15	39	40	26
Total	120	100	38	100	158	100

In this respect we find that for agreeing to completely retire from their profession at 70 years of age by elderly lawyers and 80 years of age by the elderly doctors, in Table 3.12 they expressed their reasons for the same as senility 30 (19%). Availability of the successor to their profession 42 (27%), peaceful religious life 48 (30%) and charitable service 38 (24%) after superannuation and complete retirement from the legal medical profession.

Table 3.12 : Reasons for Complete Retirement Among the Elderly Lawyers and Doctors

Reasons	*Elderly Lawyers*		*Elderly Doctors*		*Total*	
	f	%	*f*	%	*f*	%
Senility	25	20	05	13	30	19
Availability of the successor to the Profession	27	23	15	39	42	27
Peaceful Religious life	38	32	10	26	48	30
Charitable social service	30	25	08	22	38	24
Total	120	100	38	100	158	100

In this way we find the socio-economic profile of the respondents is full of varieties of facets and views about aging its relative problems and ways of adjustment and reconciliation on the part of different categories of respondents.

4 AGING AND SOCIO-CULTURAL ADJUSTMENTS

The social structure defines roles considered appropriate for its older members. What types of adjustments or relations these roles may require, how justified these role definitions are from the perspective of the aging individual and his/her basic human rights, what difficulties the elderly may face, what appropriate social mechanisms might be required to minimise the stresses and strains of aging and to maximise the potential for making aging a worthy and enjoyable life experience are the chief considerations in social cultural adjustments while facing the aging problems in the contemporary changing social scenario.

The identified social structural variables which are expected to make a difference to the condition of the elderly are : age, sex, economic condition, occupational status, education, family structure, location differences and religious background. These are a few of the background characteristics of an elderly person, based on sociological perspective of the aging problems.

If viewed in the context of changing social system the framework of social structure including its related concepts of social position, role and status, the aging problem would consist in the difficulties experienced by the elderly in maintaining their status while changing positions and roles in old age. The Indian society at present is transforming itself into industrial social order in which old people have to fall back upon their own achievements in filling new roles. They are thus exposed to the vulnerability of the aging process from which they were shielded in the pre-industrial social order hence needing very many social cultural adjustments due to the aging at present. In their efforts toward socio-cultural adjustment, the superannuated and elderly shall have to compromise and reconcile with the replaced, substituted and innovated novel social institutions values and norms. Further the elderly have to take many wise decisions and come out successful facing the existing state of social anomy of lawlessness, normlessness, and a sort of moral vacuum while making adjustment with the aging problems at present. In the wake of weakening of specially the traditional joint/extended family in India formerly providing the bulk of care, support and attributing due status and honour to the older family members, the senior citizens have now been left to their own fate alone to make suitable social and cultural adjustments to the aging problems.

Nature of Family Relations

Table 4.1 shows the nature of family relations of the respondents on four counts, viz. cordial, normal, uncordial and very strained. On the whole we find impact on family relations as reported by 70, 22, 01 and 07 per cent respectively indicating cordial, normal, uncordial and very strained. The distribution of the consequences of aging on family relations per categorywise respondents is as 28 (67%), 8 (19%), and 6 (14%) reporting cordial, normal and very strained ones respectively among the superannuated university teachers; as 35 (88%), 04 (10%), and 01 (2 %) reporting cordial, normal and uncordial family relations respectively among the superannuated civil servants, as 75 (63%), 35 (29%), 02 (01 %) and 8 (7%) reporting cordial, normal, uncordial and very strained family relations respectively among the elderly lawyers, similarly as 30 (79%), 05 (13%), 03 (08%) reporting cordial, normal and very strained family relations respectively among the elderly doctors.

Table 4.1 : Nature of Family Relations

Nature of Family Relations	*Superannuated University Teachers*		*Superannuated Civil Servants*		*Elderly Lawyers*		*Elderly Doctors*		*Total*	
	f	*%*	*f*	*%*	*f*	*%*	*f*	*%*	*f*	*%*
Cordial	28	67	35	88	75	63	30	79	70	81
Normal	08	19	04	10	35	29	05	13	52	22
Uncordial	–	–	01	02	02	01	-	-	03	01
Very Strained	06	14	–	–	08	07	03	08	17	07
Total	42	100	40	100	120	100	38	100	240	100

This shows that family relations are predominantly cordial, i.e. 168 (70%) among all the categories of respondents. Aging could adversely affect family relations of the respondents to the extent of 3 (01%) uncordial and 17 (7%) very strained ones.

Children Away from the Parental Home

Sometimes grown up children do not stay with their elderly parents because of various unavoidable reasons. In this respect in Table 4.2 we find as 05 (2%), 28 (12%), 162 (68%), 10 (4%) and 35 (14%) reporting respectively for reasons like stepmother in the home, daughter married, sons employed at far off places, shortage of accommodation and children studying elsewhere.

Table 4.2 : Reasons for Children Not Living with the Respondents

Reasons	*Superannuated University Teachers*		*Superannuated Civil Servants*		*Elderly Lawyers*		*Elderly Doctors*		*Total*	
	f	*%*	*f*	*%*	*f*	*%*	*f*	*%*	*f*	*%*
Step-mother	–	–	–	–	05	04	–	–	05	02
Daughters married	06	14	04	10	15	12	03	08	28	12
Sons employed at far off places	30	72	32	80	70	58	30	79	162	68
Shortage of accommodation	–	–	–	–	10	28	–	–	10	24
Children studying elsewhere	06	14	04	10	20	16	05	13	35	14
	42	100	40	100	120	100	38	100	–	–
Total	42	18	40	17	120	50	38	15	240	100

Among the categorywise respondents the distribution of different reasons is as 6 (14%), 30 (72%), and 6 (14%) respectively for daughters married, sons employed at far off places and children studying elsewhere among the superannuated university teachers as 4 (10%), 32 (80%), and 4 (10%) respectively for daughter married, sons employed at far off places and children studying, elsewhere among the superannuated civil servants, as 5 (4%), 15 (12%), 70 (50%), 10 (8%), and 20 (16%) respectively for reasons of stepmother in home, daughters married, sons employed at far off places, shortage of accommodation and children studying elsewhere among the elderly lawyers, similarly as 3 (8%), 30 (79%), and 5 (13%) respectively for daughters married sons employed at far off places and children studying elsewhere among the elderly doctors.

Modes of Contact with Native Family by Outstation Family Members

In modern age of industrialization and urbanization due to

opportunities for higher studies and jobs in distant big cities young family members prefer their study at those far off places and this step has resulted into various problems to the elderly parents left alone at the native home uncared and none to look after them. If these outstation family members retain and maintain contact with their elderly parents at the native home by regularly visiting and remitting money and gifts etc. to the elderly parents, then this will definitely give sufficient solace and emotional security to the elderly people.

In this respect Table 4.3 shows many modes of maintaining contact with the native family and elderly parents as personal visit from time to time, sending letters and remitting gifts and money and telephonic talks. There are eight (08) such cases among the elderly lawyers who report that their outstation younger family members never think of establishing contact by any mode so far. The rest of the respondents of all the four categories report either of the four modes mentioned above by their outstation family members. We find the distribution of these different modes of contact as reported by 105 (44%), 58 (24%), 28 (12%) and 41 (17%) respectively for personal visit, sending letters, remittances and gifts and telephonic talks by outstation family members.

Table 4.3 : Ways of Establishing Contact with the Native Family by the Outstation Family Members

Ways of contact with Native Family	*Superannuated University Teachers*		*Superannuated Civil Servants*		*Elderly Lawyers*		*Elderly Doctors*		*Total*	
	f	%	*f*	%	*f*	%	*f*	%	*f*	%
Personal visit	30	48	30	76	50	42	05	13	105	44
Letters	10	24	05	12	43	36	–	–	58	24
Remittance and Presents	10	24	05	12	10	08	03	08	28	12
Telephonic contact	02	04	–	–	09	07	30	79	41	17
Not Establishing Any Contact with the Native Family	–	–	–	–	08	07	–	–	08	03
	42	100	40	100	120	100	38	100	–	–
Total	42	18	40	17	120	50	38	15	240	100

As per categorywise respondents we find different ways of establishing contact with the native family by outstation family members as 20 (48%), 10 (24%), 10 (24%), and 02 (4%) respectively for personal visit, sending letters remittances and gifts and having telephonic talks, reported by the superannuated university teachers, as 30 (76%), 5 (12%) and 5 (12%) respectively for personal visit, letters and remittances and gifts etc. reported by superannuated civil servants, as 50 (42%), 43 (36%), 10 (8%) and 9 (7%) respectively for personal visit, letters, remittances and gifts and telephonic talk reported by elderly lawyers and as: 5 (13%), 3 (8%) and 30 (79%) respectively for personal visit, remittances and gifts and telephonic contact reported by the elderly doctors.

Feeling Social Alienation

The feeling of social alienation is both a cause and consequence of aging problems to the senior citizens. Strange enough in Table 4.4 we find about 194 (81%) respondents reporting not at all any such feeling of social alienation. Those, who feel social alienation, are distributed as 30 (16%), 32 (16%), 100 (52%) and 32 (16%) respectively among the superannuated university teachers, civil servants, elderly lawyers and doctors.

Table 4.4 : Feeling Social Alienation

Social Alienation Feeling	*Superannuated University Teachers*		*Superannuated Civil Servants*		*Elderly Lawyers*		*Elderly Doctors*		*Total*	
	f	%	*f*	%	*f*	%	*f*	%	*f*	%
Sometime	10	24	-7	17	11	09	04	10	32	13
Most of the time	02	04	01	03	09	08	02	05	14	06
Never	30	72	32	80	100	83	32	85	194	81
	42	100	40	100	120	100	38	100	–	–
Total	42	18	40	17	120	50	38	15	240	100

As regards feeling social alienation on two counts, viz. 'sometimes' and 'Most of the times' among the different categories of respondents we find the distribution of their respondent as: 10 (24%), and 02 (4%) respectively for sometimes and most of the time among the superannuated university teachers, as 7 (17%), and 1 (3%) respectively for sometimes and most of the time among the superannuated civil servants, as 11 (9%) and 9 (8%) respectively for sometimes and most of the time among the elderly lawyers; as 4 (10%) and 2 (5%) respectively for sometimes and most of the time among the elderly doctors.

Reasons for Social Alienation Feeling

Many reasons have been stated by the respondents for the feeling of social alienation. 46 respondents feeling socially alienated have furnished reasons as 21(46%), 8 (17%), 9 (20%) and 8 (17%) respectively for contemptuous attitude of family members, conflicting values, adverse relations and minimum relations with others: the distribution as per categorywise respondents in Table 4.5 we find 5 (42%), 4 (33%) and 3 (25%) respectively for contemptuous attitude of family members, adverse and minimum relations with others among the superannuated university teachers, as 4 (50%), 2 (36%), 1 (12 %) and 1 (12%) respectively for contemptuous attitude of family members, conflicting values, adverse and minimum relations with others among the superannuated civil servants, as 9 (45%), 5 (25%), 4 (20%), and 2 (10%) respectively for contemptuous attitude of family members; conflicting values, adverse and minimum relations with others among the elderly lawyers, as 3 (50%), 1 (17%) and 2 (33%) respectively for contemptuous attitude of family members, conflicting values and minimum relations with others among the elderly doctors.

Table 4.5 : Reasons for Feeling Social Alienation

Reasons	*Superannuated University Teachers*		*Superannuated Civil Servants*		*Elderly Lawyers*		*Elderly Doctors*		*Total*	
	f	*%*	*f*	*%*	*f*	*%*	*f*	*%*	*f*	*%*
Contemptuous attitude of Family members	05	42	04	50	09	45	03	50	21	46
Conflicting values	–	–	02	26	05	25	01	17	08	17
Adverse Relations	04	33	01	12	04	20	–	–	09	20
Minimum Relations with others	03	25	01	12	02	10	02	33	08	17
Total	12	100	08	100	20	100	06	100	46	100

Expecting the Nature of Support from Children in Old Age

The superannuated and elderly persons may need some sort of support from their children in their old age but in this respect we find a good number of such respondents, i.e. 73 (31%), who do not like or expect any sort of help from their children in Table 4.6. The categorywise

Table 4.6 : Expecting Support from the Children

Support	*Superannuated University Teachers*		*Superannuated Civil Servants*		*Elderly Lawyers*		*Elderly Doctors*		*Total*	
	f	*%*	*f*	*%*	*f*	*%*	*f*	*%*	*f*	*%*
Physical	02	04	01	02	15	12	–	–	18	07
Monetary	02	04	03	08	15	12	–	–	20	08
Emotional	25	61	24	60	60	50	20	53	129	54
Expecting no help of any sort	13	31	12	30	30	26	18	47	73	31
	42	100	40	100	120	100	38	100	–	–
Total	42	18	40	17	120	50	38	15	240	100

distribution of these respondents is 13 (31%), 12 (30%), 30 (26%) and 18 (47%) respectively for superannuated teachers, civil servants, elderly lawyers and doctors.

Those expecting support from their children they need physical, monetary and emotional support. On the whole the distribution of these required support as reported by 18 (7%), 20(8%), and 12 (54%) respectively for physical, monetary and emotional support. The distribution as per categorywise respondents is as 2 (4%), 2 (4%) and 25 (10%) respectively for physical, monetary and emotional support among the superannuated university teachers, as 1(2%), 3(8%) and 24 (60%) respectively for physical, monetary and emotional support among the superannuated civil servants, as 15 (12%), 15 (12%), and 60 (50%) respectively for physical, monetary and emotional support among the elderly lawyers, as only 20 (53%) need emotional support among the elderly doctors.

Persons Looking after the Elderly in the Family in Old Age

It is a popular belief that in old age the elderly generally depend on their sons/grandsons. In case they do not have their own sons/grandsons then the relatives are requested to look after them. There is none else to depend in old age except the above two categories. In Table 4.7 we find mostly respondents 155 (65%) report none to look-after them in old age. These unfortunate face the tune of fast aging problems themselves. They deserve due sympathy and sweet care by the governmental as well as non-governmental agencies after superannuation or 60 years of age. They are helpless hence if young family members also disown them, only alternative is then government run

Old Age Home and Day Care centre etc. Further very few fortunate respondents, i.e. 30 (12%) enjoy their sons'/grandsons' care in old age. The rest of the respondents, i.e. 55 (23%) are looked after by some of their relatives.

Table 4.7 : Persons Looking After the Elderly on Supperannuation or After 60 Years of Age

Persons looking after the elderly	*Superannuated University Teachers*		*Superannuated Civil Servants*		*Elderly Lawyers*		*Elderly Doctors*		*Total*	
	f	%	*f*	%	*f*	%	*f*	%	*f*	%
Sons/ Grand sons	4	10	6	15	16	13	04	11	30	15
Relatives	13	31	12	30	30	25	–	–	55	23
None	25	59	22	55	74	62	34	89	155	65
Total	42	100	40	100	120	100	38	100	240	100

In the categorywise distribution in respect of elderly doctors there is a reporting by 34 (89%) respondents as None to lookafter them. This is so only because the elderly doctors are socially and economically so well off that they need none to lookafter them in their old age. There are only 4 doctor respondents who admit that they are well looked after by their sons. As regards superannuated university teachers the distribution is as 4(10%), 13 (31%) and 25 (59%) respectively for sons/grandsons; relatives and none; similarly in case of superannuated civil servants the distribution is as 6(15%), 12 (30%), and 22 (55%) respectively for sons/grandsons, relatives and none. In case of elderly lawyers we find as 16(13%), 30(25%) and 74(62%) respectively for sons/grandsons, relatives and none.

Liking for the Person with whom to Converse with

It is generally found that elderly people would prefer a person to converse with some one who is most intimate, close and favourite to them. In this respect we find some types of persons such as spouse, children, grandchildren, Relatives, Neightbours and friends etc., the elderly may choose either of them for conversation. In this connection in Table 4.8 we find the distribution of the preference for the person for conversation as 180(75%), 19(8%), 31(13%), 5(02%) and 5(02%) respectively on the whole for spouse, children, grandchildren, Relatives, Neighbours/friends. The distribution among the different categories of respondents is as 30(71%), 02(5%) and 10(24%)

respectively for spouse, children and Grand children among the superannuated university teachers; as 35 (88%), 02(5%), and 3(7%) respectively for spouse, children and grandchildren among the superannuated civil servants, as 85(71%), 10(8%), 15(13%), 5(4%) and 5(4%) respectively for spouse, children, grandchildren, relatives and Neighbours/friends among the elderly lawyers, as 30 (79%), 5(13%) and 3(8%) respectively for spouse, children, and grandchildren among the elderly doctors. Generally the respondents, i.e. 180 (75%) prefer spouse to converse with treating him/her most dependable and intimate.

Table 4.8 : Prefer to Converse with Whom

Converse with	*Superannuated University Teachers*		*Superannuated Civil Servants*		*Elderly Lawyers*		*Elderly Doctors*		*Total*	
	f	*%*	*f*	*%*	*f*	*%*	*f*	*%*	*f*	*%*
Spouse	30	7!	35	88	85	71	30	79	180	75
Children	02	05	02	05	10	08	05	13	19	08
Grand children	10	24	03	07	15	13	03	08	31	13
Relatives	–	–	–	–	05	04	–	–	05	02
Neighbour and Friend	–	–	–	–	05	04	–	–	05	02
	42	100	40	100	120	100	38	100		
Total	42	18	40	17	120	50	38	15	240	100

Participation in Family Functions

The elderly people generally like to participate in the family functions from time to time or on occasions but there are 10(40%), such respondents in Table 4.9 who do not participate in the family functions.

Table 4.9 : Participation in Family Functions

Participation	*Superannuated University Teachers*		*Superannuated Civil Servants*		*Elderly Lawyers*		*Elderly Doctors*		*Total*	
	f	*%*	*f*	*%*	*f*	*%*	*f*	*%*	*f*	*%*
Always	30	71	35	88	85	71	25	66	175	73
Most of the Time	09	22	03	08	20	17	10	26	42	18
Sometimes	01	02	02	04	10	08	–	–	13	05
Never	02	05	–	–	05	04	03	08	10	04
	42	100	40	100	120	100	38	100		
Total	42	18	40	17	120	50	38	15	240	100

These respondents are distributed as 2 (50%), nil, 5 (4%), 3 (8%) respectively for superannuated university teachers, civil servants, elderly lawyers and doctors. The rest of the respondents generally participate in the family functions and the nature of their participation is on the whole as 175 (73%), 42 (18%), and 13 (5%) respectively for always, most of the time and sometimes. as per categorywise respondents the distribution of the nature of participation is as 30(71%), 9(22%), and 1(2%) respectively for always, most of the times and sometimes among the superannuated university teachers as 35(88%), 03(8%), and 2(4%) respectively for always, most of the time and sometimes among the superannuated civil servants, as 85(70%), 20(17%), and 10(8%) respectively for always, most of the time and sometimes among the elderly lawyers as 25 (66%), 10(26%) respectively for always, and most of the time among the elderly doctors.

Reasons for Not Attending Family Functions

The ten (10) respondents distributed as 2, 5, and 03 respectively among superannuated university teachers elderly lawyers and doctors, have disclosed some of their reasons for not attending family functions. The distribution of these reasons among all the ten (10) respondents is as 6 (60%), 1 (10%), 1(10%), and 2(20%) respectively for avoiding family bickering, unwelcoming attitude of the family members, considering it an expensive affair and ill health of the self in Table 4.10.

Table 4.10 : Reasons for not Attending Family Functions

Reasons	*Superannuated University Teachers*		*Superannuated Civil Servants*		*Elderly Lawyers*		*Elderly Doctors*		*Total*	
	f	%	*f*	%	*f*	%	*f*	%	*f*	%
To avoid family bickering	01	50	–	–	02	40	03	100	06	60
Unwelcoming attitude of the family members	–	–	–	–	01	20	–	–	01	10
Considering an expensive affair	–	–	–	–	01	20	–	–	01	10
Ill health of the self	01	50	–	–	01	20	–	–	02	20
	02	100		100	05	100	03	100	10	
Total	02	20	–	–	05	50	03	30	10	100

Honour and Obedience from Family Member after Superannuation or 60 Years of Age

While assessing the honour and obedience enjoyed by the elderly from young family members we find 58(24%) respondents report receiving honour and obedience by young members in Table 4.11. About 130 (55%) report Never enjoying honour and obedience from their young family members. On the other hand there are about 58(24°%) fortunate respondents still receiving honour and obedience from their young family members. There are few about 20(8%) respondents report such an honour and obedience only sometimes and 32(13%) only often.

Table 4.11 : Honour and Obedience from Family members After Superannuation or 60 Years of Age

Honour and Obedience from Family members	*Superannuated University Teachers*		*Superannuated Civil Servants*		*Elderly Lawyers*		*Elderly Doctors*		*Total*	
	f	*%*	*f*	*%*	*f*	*%*	*f*	*%*	*f*	*%*
Always	03	07	02	05	15	12	38	100	58	24
Sometimes	07	17	10	25	03	03	–	–	20	08
Often	05	12	02	05	25	21	–	–	32	13
Never	27	64	26	65	77	64	–	–	130	55
Total	42	100	40	100	120	100	38	100	240	100

The categorywise distribution of honour and obedience from young family members toward the elderly is as 23(7%), 7(17%), 05(12%), 7(4%) respectively for always, sometimes, often and never among the superannuated university teachers as 2(5%), 10(25%), 02(05%), and 26 (65%) respectively among the superannuated civil servants, as 15 (12%), 3 (3%), 25(21%) and 77 (64%) respectively for always, sometimes, often and never among the elderly lawyers.

The only category of elderly doctors respondents who without any exception all enjoy honour and receive obedience from their younger family members.

Respondent's Reaction to Dishonour and Disobedience from Younger Family Members

Aging problem becomes much acute if the superannuated/elderly respondents are denied of due honour and find disobedience from younger family members. 'The only reaction to such situation is a sort of irritation and depression among the superannuated and elderly respondent and except the elderly doctors. Hence Table 4.12 shows the reaction among the rest of the categories of the respondents i.e. superannuated university teachers, civil servants and elderly lawyers. On the whole this reaction is found us 17(08%), 88(43%) and 97(49%) respectively for remaining always irritated, sometimes irritated, never irritated. The highest percentage among the respondents 97(49%) is for never irritated. There we find the patience and ways of reconciliation with most disrespectful consequence of aging among the three categories of respondents i.e. superannuated university teaches 12(08%), civil servants 15(37%) and elderly lawyers 70(58%).

Table 4.12 : Reaction toward Dishonour and Disobedience from Younger Family Member

Reaction	*Superannuated University Teachers*		*Superannuated Civil Servants*		*Elderly Lawyers*		*Elderly Doctors*		*Total*	
	f	*%*	*f*	*%*	*f*	*%*	*f*	*%*	*f*	*%*
Remain always irriated	05	12	02	05	10	09	–	–	17	98
Sometime irritated	25	60	23	58	40	33	–	–	88	43
Never irriated	12	28	15	37	70	58	–	–	97	49
Total	42	100	40	100	120	100	–	–	202	100

Modes of Reconciliation and Compromise

There are number of ways for reconciliation with dishonour and disobedience if shown by the younger family members, such as yielding. keeping mum. Least interference with family matters. Becoming submissive even to younger family members and keeping himself away from the house especially when there is a fear of quarrel or bickering in the house.

On the whole modes of reconciliation if dishonour and disobedience shown by younger family members, are as 25(11%), 136(57%), 67(28%), 6(2%), and 6(2%) respectively for yielding, keeping mum, least interference in family matters, becoming submissive and passive before younger family members and keeping him/herself away from the house for sometime in Table 4.13. This shows how pitiable condition of the majority of respondents, i.e.

Table 4.13 : Mode of Reconciliation with Dishonour and Disobedience from Family Members

Mode of Reconciliation	*Superannuated University Teachers*		*Superannuated Civil Servants*		*Elderly Lawyers*		*Elderly Doctors*		*Total*	
	f	*%*	*f*	*%*	*f*	*%*	*f*	*%*	*f*	*%*
Yielding	10	24	05	13	10	08	–	–	25	11
Keeping Mum	30	71	28	70	70	59	08	21	136	57
Least interference with family matters	02	05	05	13	30	25	30	79	67	28
Becoming submissive and passing before younger family members	–	–	01	02	05	04	–	–	06	02
Keeping away self from the house for some time	–	–	01	02	05	04	–	–	06	02
Total	42	100	40	100	120	100	38	100	240	100

136(57%), prefer keeping mum as a mode of reconciliation with the neglective attitude of the younger family members.

The distribution as per categorywise respondents is as: 10(24%), 30(71%), and 2(5%) respectively for yielding, keeping mum, and least interference in family matters as modes of reconciliation among the superannuated university teachers, as: 5(13%), 28(70%), 5(13%), 01(2%), and 01(2%), respectively for yielding, keeping mum, least interference with family matters, becoming, submissive and passive before younger family members and keeping him/herself away from house for sometime among the superannuated civil servants; as: 10(8%), 70(59%), 30(25%), 05(4%), and 5(4%) respectively for yielding, keeping mum, least interference with family matters, becoming submissive and passive before younger family members, keeping him/herself away from the house for sometime among the elderly lawyers; as: 8(21%) and 30(79%) respectively for keeping mum and least interference with family matters among the elderly doctors.

Frequency of Meeting with Friends/Neighbours (Before and After Superannuation or 60 years of Age)

The analysis of the frequency of meeting and mixing with friends/

neighbours etc. reflects the degree of respondents tie with the social bound, i.e. their involvement with social interaction and the extent of social alienation. The higher the degree of frequency of mixing and meeting with the people in the community the more it shall be a potent source of coping with many aging problems. Here in Table 4.14 we compare the degree of frequency of respondents meeting and mixing with the friends/neighbours etc. before and after superannuation and 60 years of age.

Before and after superannuation and 60 years of age we find as : 50(21%), 26(11%), 131(55%) and 33(13%) (Before) and 15(6%), 24(10%), 163(68%) and 38(16%) (After) respectively for more frequently, frequently, less frequently and hardly ever meeting. Here we find that the frequency of respondents meeting and mixing with the neighbours/friends has decreased after superannuation and 60 years of age less frequently meeting before superannuation and 60 years of age as 131(55%) and after superannuation and 60 years of age it is 163(68%) such a situation shall make the respondents more helpless in facing aging problems because of the increase in the degree of social alienation and decrease in the degree of tie with the social bond.

Further the distribution as per different categories of respondents we find 35(84%), 5(12%), 1(2%), and 1(2%) (before) and 5(12%), 4(10%), 23(55%) and 10(23%) (after) superannuation and 60 years of age respectively for more frequently, frequently, less frequently and hardly ever meeting among the superannuated teachers; as: (Before) 5(12%), 5(12%), 30(76%) respectively for more frequently, frequently and less frequently and (after) as 35(88%), and 5(12%) respectively for less frequently and hardly ever meeting among the superannuated civil servants; as: (before): 10(8%), 12(10%), 70(58%), and 28(24%), and (After) as 10(8%), 20(16%), 70(58%), and 20(18%) respectively for more frequently, frequently, less frequently and hardly ever meeting among the elderly lawyers; as (before): 4(11%), 230(78%) and 4(11%) respectively for frequently, less frequently and hardly ever meeting and (after), as: 35(92%) and 3(8%) respectively for less frequently and hardly ever meeting among the elderly doctors.

Issues of Conversation on Meeting with Friends and Neighbours

The important issues or topics for conversation, gossip and discussion while meeting with friends and neighbours are generally family

Table 4.14 : Frequency of Meeting with Friends and Neighbours Before and After Superannuation or 60 Years of Age

Frequency of meeting	*Superannuated University Teachers*				*Superannuated Civil Servants*				*Elderly Lawyers*				*Elderly Doctors*				*Total*			
	Before		*After*		*Before*		*After*		*Before*		*After*		*Before*		*After*		*Before*		*After*	
	f	*%*	*f*	*%*	*f*	*%*	*f*	*%*	*f*	*%*	*f*	*%*	*f*	*%*	*f*	*%*	*f*	*%*	*f*	*%*
More frequently	35	54	05	12	05	12	–	–	10	08	10	08	–	–	–	–	50	21	15	06
Frequently	05	12	04	10	05	12	–	–	12	10	20	16	04	11	–	–	26	11	24	10
Less Frequently	01	02	23	55	30	76	35	88	70	58	70	58	30	78	35	92	131	55	163	68
Hardly ever meeting	01	02	10	23	–	–	05	12	28	24	20	18	04	11	03	08	33	13	38	16
Total	42	100	42	100	40	100	40	100	120	100	120	100	38	100	38	100	240	100	240	100

Table 4.15 : Main Issues of Conversation of meeting with Friends and Neighbours After Superannuation or 60 years of Age

Issues of conversation	*Superannuated University Teachers*		*Superannuated Civil Servants*		*Elderly Lawyers*		*Elderly Doctors*		*Total*	
	f	%	*f*	%	*f*	%	*f*	%	*f*	%
Family matter	30	71	25	64	15	13	04	10	74	31
Declining social values	02	05	05	12	18	15	–	–	25	10
Economic problem	05	12	05	12	12	10	–	–	22	09
Religious Discussion	–	–	–	–	15	13	04	10	19	08
Professional issues	–	–	–	–	50	41	30	80	80	33
Social Security problem	05	12	05	12	10	08	–	–	20	09
Total	42	100	40	100	120	100	38	100	240	100

matters, declining social values, economic problems, religious topics, professional issues and lastly social security problems. On the whole in Table 4.15 among all the respondents we find distribution of issues, topics and items of conversation with friends and neighbours by the superannuated and elderly respondents as: 74(31%), 25(10%), 22(9%), 19(08%), 80(33%), and 20(9%) respectively for family matters, declining social values, economic problem, religious discussion, professional issues and social security problems.

The distribution according to the respective category of respondents is as: 30(71%), 2(5%), 05(12%) respectively for family matter, declining social values and economic problem among the superannuated university teachers, as: 25(64%), 5(12%) and 5(12%) respectively for family matter, declining social values and economic problem, among the superannuated civil servants, as: 15(13%), 18(15%), 12(10%), 15(13%), 50(41%), and 10(8%) respectively for family matters, declining social values, economic problem, religious discussion, professional issues and social security problems among the elderly lawyers and as: 4(10%), 4(10%) and 30(80%) respectively for family matter, religious matter and professional issues among the elderly doctors.

Conclusion

The sociological perspective approach, envisaged as the main thrust of the present study, has been widely applied here in various of its dimensions of aging problems such as the nature of family relations, the extent of social bond, the feeling of social alienation, Active and Passive as well as optimistic and pessimistic ways of respondents involvement in social interaction, conciliatory and conflicting attitudes between the elderly respondents and younger family members and lastly locating persons on whom the elderly respondents would like to depend and have close and intimate contact etc.

There is a coincidence of age and social structure and if there develops a sort of disbalance and contrary situations in between physical aging and allotment of roles, position and power to the elderly in the social set up due to the contemporary social forces of urbanization, industrialization, modernization, globalization and politicization, then the elderly are compelled to make many sorts of social cultural adjustments in order to maintain the social order.

In this effort for making many possible adjustment with the changing social scenario some elderly respondents experience many difficulties in reconciling with the current unexpected changes in the social norms, values, attitudes and functioning of the basic social institutions. All these various facets have been examined and valuable findings obtained. In order to maintain a strong social order many sort of social-cultural adjustments are highly needed for setting the balance right between age and social structure.

5 AGING AND ECONOMIC ADJUSTMENTS

The senior citizens after superannuation or attaining 60 years of age have to face the first and foremost aging problem of economic loss and its adjustment. The superannuated elderly start receiving pension of meagre amount in place of regular salary of sumptuous nature. The superannuated have to bear with this economic loss every month and they immediately start searching alternative remunerative job/work/ profession and make many adjustments to their day to day life for the future security.

On the other hand those elderly persons engaged in legal and medical professions also suffer some economic loss due to physical aging after attaining sixty years of age although they are not bound with any mandatory retirement age. It is their sweet will to decide when to slow down their active involvement or completely give up practising their respective profession. In order to assess their economic problem if any with them can be derived by comparing shifts and changes in their income groups before and after attaining sixty years of age. They make economic adjustments as a result of falling and rising trend of their income groups after attaining 60 years of age.

In this way the respondents of both the categories viz. superannuated mandatory retired and nonsuperannuated non-mandatory privately running professional respondents have to make economic adjustment after mandatory retirement or nonmandatory age of 60 years, i.e. due to physical aging.

In the process of economic adjustment many important aspects and efforts are worth probing into such as views about continuity and discontinuity of job/profession/work, changes in income groups before and after sixty years of age; Adequacy of the present income; manipulated additional sources of income after sixty years of age, sources on which to fall back upon in times of need and emergency, sources of social and economic security for the old age etc.

Table 5.1 : Considerations for Continuing Profession/Job After Superannuation or 60 Years of Age

Consideration	*Superannuated University Teachers*		*Superannuated Civil Servants*		*Elderly Lawyers*		*Elderly Doctors*		*Total*	
	f	%	*f*	%	*f*	%	*f*	%	*f*	%
Good health	30	71	28	70	75	63	30	79	163	68
Financial need	–	–	04	10	25	21	–	–	29	12
A Sort of engagement	08	19	06	15	–	–	06	16	20	08
Retaining Social Status	02	05	–	–	05	04	–	–	07	03
Yet Not free from Liabilities	–	–	–	–	10	08	–	–	10	04
Not at all continuing	02	05	02	05	05	04	02	05	11	05
Total	42	100	40	100	120	100	38	100	240	100

Views About Continuing Profession/Job/Work After Superannuation or 60 years of Age

As regards respondents' views about continuing profession/ job/ work even after superannuation or 60 years of age we find their distribution in Table 5.1 on the whole is as: 163(68%), 29(12%), 20(8%), 7(30%) and 10 (4%) respectively for good health, financial need, a sort of engagement, retaining social status, not yet free from liabilities. On the other hand there are 11 (50%) such respondents who favour discontinuity of work/job/profession after 60 years of age and superannuation. These 11 cases are distributed as 2(5%), 2(5%), 5(4%) and 2(5%) respectively among superannuated university teachers, civil servants, elderly lawyers and doctors.

The distribution of various considerations of the respondents for maintaining continuity to profession is as: 30 (71%), 8 (19%), and 2(5%) respectively for good heath, a sort of engagement and retaining social status among the superannuated university teachers; as: 28 (76%), 4(10%) and 6 (15%) respectively for good health; financial need, and a sort of engagement among the superannuated civil servants; as: 75 (63%), 25 (21%), 5 (4%) and 10 (8%) respectively for good health, financial need, retaining social status and not free from liabilities among the elderly lawyers, as: 30 (79%) and 6 (16%)

respectively for good health and a sort of engagement among the elderly doctors.

The dominant consideration is good health, i.e. 163 (68%) for continuing the profession/job and work. The distribution of the respondents holding this consensus view of good health is as 30 (71%) superannuated university teachers, 28(70%) superannuated civil servants, 75 (63%) elderly lawyers and 30 (79%) elderly doctors.

Table 5.2 : Consequences if Discontinuity of Profession/Job After Superannuation or 60 Years of Age

Consequences	*Superannuated University Teachers*		*Superannuated Civil Servants*		*Elderly Lawyers*		*Elderly Doctors*		*Total*	
	f	*%*	*f*	*%*	*f*	*%*	*f*	*%*	*f*	*%*
Fast Aging	02	05	05	13	50	42	05	13	62	26
Depression	05	12	05	13	30	25	03	08	38	16
Worry and Tension	02	05	05	13	20	17	–	–	27	11
Loss of economic status	–	–	–	–	10	08	–	–	15	06
Loss of social status	04	09	–	–	04	03	–	–	08	04
Feeling of social alienation	05	12	–	–	–	–	–	–	05	02
Search for an alternative job/ profession	05	12	–	–	–	–	–	–	05	02
None of the above consequences	19	45	25	61	06	05	30	74	80	33
Total	42	100	40	100	120	100	38	100	240	100

Consequences of Discontinuity of Profession/Job After Superannuation or 60 years of Age

The bad consequences follow if there is discontinuity of the remunerative job/work/profession such as fast aging, depression, worry and tension, dependency due to loss of economic status, loss of social status, feeling of social alienation and a search for an alternative remunerative job/work/profession etc.

In Table 5.2 we find a good number, i.e. 80 (33%) respondents experiencing no bad consequence of discontinuity of work/job/ profession. These respondents are distributed as 19 (45%), 25 (61%), 6 (5%) and 30 (79%) respectively for superannuated university teachers, civil servants, elderly lawyers and doctors. This shows that the discontinuity of work/job/profession does not adversely affect the elderly doctors (79%) and superannuated civil servants (61%).

In respect of the rest of the respondents the distribution of the evil consequences of the discontinuity of work/job/profession as reported is as : 62 (26%), 38 (16%), 27 (11%), 15 (06%), 8 (4%), 5 (2%), and 5 (2%) respectively for fast aging. Depression, worry and tension, loss of economic status, loss of social status, feeling of social alienation and search for an alternative remunerative/non-remunerative job/work/profession.

As per categorywise respondents we find the distribution of the reported consequences of discontinuity of work/job/profession in modern age is as : 2 (5%), 5 (12%), 2(5%), 4(9%), 5(12%) and again 5 (12%) respectively for fast aging depression. Worry, tension, loss of economic status, loss of social status, feeling of social alienation and search for an alternative job/work/profession among the superannuated university teachers; as: 5(13%), 5 (13%) and 5 (13%) respectively for fast aging. Depression and worry and tension among the superannuated civil servants, as 50 (42%), 30 (25%), 20 (17%), 10 (8%) and 4 (3%) respectively for fast aging, depression, worry and tension, loss of economic status and loss of social status among the elderly lawyers; as 5 (13%) and 3 (8%) respectively for fast aging and depression among the elderly doctors.

Loss in the Economic Status

The assessment of the loss and gain in the economic status to the respondents has been attempted in Table 5.4 on income groups of the respondents before and after superannuation or 60 years of age under Chapter III on 'Socio-economic profile of the respondents'. In this table on comparing the distribution of income groups of the respondents before and after superannuation and 60 years of age we find rise and fall in the levels of income groups before and after superannuation or 60 years of age. In this respect we find there is definite loss in the economic status to the superannuated university teachers and civil servants because of inadequate pension amount after superannuation, being the main source of income. Comparatively there is some rise in the economic status in respect of elderly lawyers and doctors.

This rise and fall in the economic status has also been the result of additional sources of income additioned by the respondents after

Table 5.3 : Adequacy of Current Income

Adequacy of Current Income	*Superannuated University Teachers*		*Superannuated Civil Servants*		*Elderly Lawyers*		*Elderly Doctors*		*Total*	
	f	*%*	*f*	*%*	*f*	*%*	*f*	*%*	*f*	*%*
Adequate	07	17	–	–	53	44	10	26	70	29
More than Adequate	–	–	–	–	12	10	28	74	40	17
Inadequate	06	14	05	12	19	16	–	–	30	12
Most inadequate	29	69	35	88	36	30	–	–	100	42
Total	42	100	40	100	120	100	38	100	240	100

superannuation or 60 years of age. The superannuated university teachers and civil servants have manipulated many additional sources of income after superannuation hence they have made the economic loss of regular salary good to some extent.

Adequacy of Current Income

An unfortunate consequence of aging problem is a sort of realisation of the current income as most inadequate.

The most unfortunate consequence of aging problem especially among the superannuated university teachers, civil servants and elderly lawyers is the realization of the reduction of the previous income to the level of considering it as most inadequate by the majority, i.e. 100 (42%). Most of the respondents, i.e. 70 (29%) do feel the current income as Adequate but 40 (17%) mostly elderly doctors and few well off elderly lawyers 12(10%) feel the present income as more than adequate. The rest 30 (12%) respondents among the superannuated university teachers, civil servants and elderly lawyers in good number realise the current income as inadequate.

In this way Table 5.3 gives an overall impression that most of the respondents, i.e. 202 have been drastically affected by the economic loss due to mandatory superannuated and crossing 60 years of age.

Additional Sources of Income after Superannuation or 60 years of Age

The respondents after superannuation and 60 years of age have arranged to manipulate some additional new sources of income in

Table 5.4 : Additional Sources of Income if Any

Additional Sources	*Superannuated University Teachers*		*Superannuated Civil Servants*		*Elderly Lawyers*		*Elderly Doctors*		*Total*	
	f	*%*	*f*	*%*	*f*	*%*	*f*	*%*	*f*	*%*
Income from Alternative job/work/profession	10	24	15	38	10	08	–	–	35	14
Hard earned savings	04	09	04	10	10	08	25	66	43	18
Financial support from children	05	12	05	12	20	16	–	–	30	13
Earning from rent of shop, land, house, and vehicles etc.	04	09	02	05	30	25	11	29	47	20
No Additional source of income	19	46	14	35	50	43	02	05	85	35
Total	42	100	40	100	120	100	38	100	240	100

order to meet the economic loss if any and make suitable adjustment. This task of searching out new additional sources of income for the superannuated and the elderly persons is a very difficult task. As in Table 5.4 we find about 85(35%) respondents distributed as 19(41%), 14(35%), 50(43%) and 2(5%) respectively among the superannuated university teachers, civil servants, elderly lawyers and doctors have failed to manipulate new additional sources of income. Naturally these respondents are not economically well off due to their failure to arrange alternative sources of income after superannuation or 60 years of age.

As per categorywise we find 10(24%), 4(9%), 5(12%) and 4(9%) the superannuated university teachers reporting respectively new sources of income as income from alternative job/work/profession, hard-earned savings, financial support front children, earning from rent of shops, land, houses and vehicles etc., as 15 (38%), 4(10%), 5(12%) and 2(5%) reporting respectively income from alternative job/work/profession, hard-earned savings, financial support from the children and earning from rent on shops, land, houses and vehicles by the superannuated civil servants; as: 10(8%), 10(8%), 20(16%) and 30(5%) reporting respectively as income from alternative job/work/profession, hard-earned savings, financial support from children, earning from rent on shops, land, houses and vehicles by the elderly lawyers; as: 25 (66%), and 11 (29%) reporting respectively for hard-earned savings, and earning from rent on shops, land, houses and vehicles by the elderly doctors.

Liabilities Remaining Unfulfilled

The other aspect of economic problem for the superannuated respondents and those attained 60 years of age is their unfulfilled liabilities. In this respect on the whole in Table 5.5 we find 90(37%) respondents reporting no liability remaining unfulfilled. These respondents are distributed in different categories as : 25 (59%) superannuated university teachers, 15(36%), superannuated civil servants, 20(17%), elderly lawyers, and 30 (79%), elderly doctors.

Table 5.5 : Unfulfilled Liabilities

Liability	*Superannuated University Teachers*		*Superannuated Civil Servants*		*Elderly Lawyers*		*Elderly Doctors*		*Total*	
	f	*%*	*f*	*%*	*f*	*%*	*f*	*%*	*f*	*%*
Education of children and Grand children	03	07	05	13	20	17	–	–	28	12
Establishing children job work	02	05	04	10	40	34	03	08	49	20
Marriage of dependent children	02	05	02	05	10	08	–	–	14	06
Building a new house, innovation of old house	–	–	–	–	10	08	05	13	15	06
Incoming expenses on cultivation work	03	07	05	13	10	08	–	–	18	08
Medical expenses	04	10	05	13	10	08	–	–	19	08
Court case expenses	03	07	04	10	–	–	–	–	07	03
No Liability unfulfilled	25	59	15	36	20	17	30	79	90	37
Total	42	100	40	100	120	100	38	100	240	100

The rest of the respondents, i.e. 150(63%), report many unfulfilled liabilities by them so far. The distribution of these unfulfilled liabilities on the whole is as : 28(12%), 49(20%), 14(6%), 15(6%), 18(5%),

19(8%), and 7(3%) respectively as education of children/grand children; establishing children in job/work profession, marriage of dependent children, building a new house/ renovation of old house, incurring expenses on agriculture, medical expenses, and court expenses.

The distribution of unfulfilled liabilities of the different categories of respondents is as: 3(7%), 2(5%), 2(5%), 3(7%), 4(10%), and 3(7%) respectively as education of children/grand children, establishing children in some job/work/profession, marriage of dependent children, incurring expenses on agriculture, medical expenses and court expenses among the superannuated university teachers; as : 5(13%), 4(10%), 2(5%), 05(13%), 5(13%) and 4(10%) respectively as education of children/grand children, establishing children in some job/work/profession, marriage of dependent children, incurring expenses on agriculture, medical expenses and court expenses among the superannuated civil servants, as: 20(17%), 40(34%), 10(8%), 10(8%), 10(8%) and 10(8%) respectively as education of children in some job/work/profession, marriage of the dependent children, building new house or renovation of old house, incurring expenses on agriculture, and medical expenses among the elderly lawyers; as: 3(8%) and 5(13%) respectively reporting establishing children in some job/work/profession, and building a new house or renovation of old house by the elderly doctors.

Security Measures for Meeting Emergency/Contingency

The elderly persons of more than 60 years of age and superannuated persons since long back before superannuation/retirement have already managed many sort of economic security measures for meeting emergency and contingency in old age after retirement or 60 years of age. These measures are mainly PF/ Gratuity, NSC/ Kissan Vikas Patra/ Recurring/ FDR in bank, LIC old Age Policy, ancestral landed and other property, Royalty/commission etc. agriculture, side business etc.

On the other hand we find a good number of respondents, i.e. 85(36%), who expressed their inability to arrange economic security measures before superannuation or 60 years of age such respondents are distributed as 19(44%), superannuated university teachers, 14(35%), superannuated civil servants, 50(43%), elderly lawyers and 2(5%) elderly doctors. Naturally these respondents always remain anxious about any emergency and contingency if takes place in old age.

The respondents who have arranged beforehand some economic security measures the distribution is as: 7(3%), 43(18%), 42(17%), 12(5%), 24(10%), 2(1%), 15(6%) and 10(4%) respectively for PF/ Gratuity, NSC/Kissan Vikas Patra/Recurring Deposit in PO; UTI Shares Dividends/Recurring and FDR in bank; LIC Old Age Policy, ancestral landed and other property, Royalty/commission etc. agriculture and side business in Table 5.6.

Table 5.6 : Security Measures for Meeting Emergency/Contingency

Security Measures	*Superannuated University Teachers*		*Superannuated Civil Servants*		*Elderly Lawyers*		*Elderly Doctors*		*Total*	
	f	*%*	*f*	*%*	*f*	*%*	*f*	*%*	*f*	*%*
PF/Gratuity	02	05	05	13	–	–	–	–	07	03
NSC/Kissan Vikas Patra/Recurring Deposit in PO	07	17	10	24	20	17	06	16	43	18
UTI Shares/ Dividends/ Recurring and FDR in Bank	07	17	05	13	10	08	20	53	42	17
LIC Old Age Policy	–	–	02	05	10	08	–	–	12	05
Ancestral Landed & other Property	02	05	02	05	10	08	10	26	24	10
Royalty/ Commission etc.	02	05	–	–	–	–	–	–	02	01
Agriculture	03	07	02	05	10	08	–	–	15	06
Side Business	–	–	–	–	10	08	–	–	10	04
No Economic Security	19	44	14	35	50	43	02	05	85	36
Total	42	100	40	100	120	100	38	100	240	100

The distribution of these economic security measures managed by the superannuated university teachers is as: 2(5%), 7(17%), 7(17%), 2(5%), 2(5%) and 3(7%) respectively for PF/Gratuity, NSC/Kissan Vikas Patra/Recurring Deposit in P.O., UTI Shares/Dividends/ Recurring and FDR in bank, ancestral landed and other properly. Royalty/commission etc., as : 5(13%), 10(24%), 5(13%), 2(5%), 2(5%), and 2(5%) respectively for PF/Gratuity, NSC/Kissan Vikas Patra/Recurring Deposit in P.O., UTI Shares/ dividends/Recurring and FDR in Bank; LIC old Age Policy, ancestral landed and other property and agriculture among the superannuated civil servants, as: 20(17%), 10(8%), 10(8%), 10(8%), 10(8%), and 10(8%) respectively for NSC/ Kissan Vikas Patra /Recurring Deposit in P.O.; UTI Shares/ dividends/ Recurring and FDR in Bank, LIC Old Age Policy, ancestral landed and other property, agriculture and side business among the elderly lawyers; as: 6(16%), 20(53%), 10(26%) respectively for NSC/ Kissan Vikas Patra/Recurring Deposit in P.O. ancestral landed and other property among the elderly doctors.

Persons Supporting the Elderly in Old Age

The superannuated senior citizens and elderly persons get support in their old age generally by their close kith and kin, relatives, friends and neighbours etc. Besides there are governmental and non-governmental agencies which also offer help and support to the elderly in facing the emergency, contingency and many other aging problems. The sorry state of affairs is that a good number of respondents, i.e. 140(58%), report that none has come forward to help and support them. Such respondents are distributed as 17(40%) superannuated university teachers, 15(37%) superannuated civil servants, 60(67%) elderly lawyers and 28(74%) elderly doctors in Table 5.7.

Table 5.7 : Persons Supporting the Elderly

Individuals Agencies Supporting Elders	*Superannuated University Teachers*		*Superannuated Civil Servants*		*Elderly Lawyers*		*Elderly Doctors*		*Total*	
	f	*%*	*f*	*%*	*f*	*%*	*f*	*%*	*f*	*%*
Children/Grand Children	–	–	–	–	20	17	10	26	30	13
Relatives	25	60	25	63	05	04	–	–	55	23
Govt./Non-Govt. Agencies	–	–	–	–	15	12	–	–	15	06
None	17	40	15	37	80	67	28	74	140	58
	N42	100	N40	100	N120	100	N38	100	N240	100

On the whole we find the distribution of those reporting some one to help and support them as: 30(13%), 55(23%), and 15(6%) respectively for children/grandchildren; relatives and governmental and non-governmental agencies. The distribution of the persons and agencies supporting the superannuated and elderly persons is as

25(60%) for relatives among the superannuated university teachers; 25(63%) for relatives again among the superannuated civil servants; as 20(17%), 5(4%), and 15(12%) respectively for children/grand-children; relatives and governmental and non-governmental agencies among the elderly lawyers, as : 10(26%) for children/grandchildren among the elderly doctors.

Expectations From the Government

As almost most of the superannuated respondents are to some extent economically depressed, hence all have some sort of expectations relating to economic relief and other support from the government. The elderly lawyers and doctors also feel some sort of economic pinch. hence being income tax payers in return they expect financial relief and many other sorts of help from the government.

Table 5.8 : Expectations from the Government

Expectations from the Government	*Superannuated University Teachers*		*Superannuated Civil Servants*		*Elderly Lawyers*		*Elderly Doctors*	
	f	*%*	*f*	*%*	*f*	*%*	*f*	*%*
Higher Pension	42	100	40	100	–	–	–	–
Income Tax Relief	42	100	40	100	80	67	20	53
Concession in Rly. and Bus Fares	42	100	40	100	90	75	–	–
Free Medical Treatment in Medical College	42	100	40	100	110	92	–	–
Mobile Dispensary	10	24	08	20	50	42	–	–
Rebate & Subsidy on Food Stuff/Gas Cylinder/K.oil	40	95	40	100	70	58	15	39
Priority in House Allotment	15	36	40	100	70	58	–	–
Tax Relief to those Helping & Looking after Elderly Parents	30	71	20	50	100	83	–	–
No Demand or expectation from the Government	–	–	–	–	–	–	10	26
Total	N-42		N-40		N-120		N-38	

As per categorywise respondents in Table 5.8 we find almost all the superannuated university teachers expect from the government: higher pension, income tax relief; concession in railway and bus fares, free medical treatment in government hospitals, 95 per cent of them expect concession and rebate etc. on food stuff and gas cylinders for fuel purpose. 71 per cent expect income tax relief to those helping their elderly parents, 36 per cent demand priority in house allotment and 24 per cent expect mobile dispensary.

Among the superannuated civil servants there is a demand by almost all from the government for higher pension, income tax relief, concessions in railway and bus fares, free medical treatment in government hospitals, concessions and rebate on food stuffs, gas cylinder, priority in house allotment, income tax relief to those helping their elderly parents by 50 per cent and mobile dispensary by 20 per cent respondents. Similarly the elderly lawyers expect from the government for free medical treatment in government hospitals by 110(92%), income tax relief to those helping their elderly parents by 100(83%), concessions in railway and bus fares by 90(75%), income tax relief to self by 80(67%), concessions and rebate on food stuff and gas cylinder, and priority in house allotment by 70(58%) and mobile dispensary by 50(42%).

Among the elderly doctors there is a demand from the government for income tax relief by 20(53%) and concessions and rebates on food stuff and gas cylinder by 15(39%). There are about 10(26%) elderly doctors much economically well off not expecting any help or support from the government.

Conclusion

On the whole we find many problems of economic adjustments before the three categories of respondents, viz. superannuated university teachers, civil servants and the elderly lawyers, but not so much for the fourth category of elderly doctors.

6 AGING AND BIO-PSYCHOLOGICAL PROBLEMS

The physical aging is a normal process with every human being. It is closely related with human body and mind. With the advancing chronological age both the structures and functioning of human organs and psychological make up of the individual gradually alter and this phenomenon is called aging or better called physical aging. These alterations can be of both intrinsic and extrinsic nature. There are varieties of such alterations and changes appear on human body as per variety of background surroundings of individual nurtures. The malignant form of such alterations and changes on body and mind produce many pathologies and diseases which need proper diagnosis and treatment. In order to carry out this task a new discipline, i.e. Gerontology has developed with its various branches such as Biological Gerontology, Psychological Gerontology and Social Gerontology.

In the present chapter with the help of the basic tenets of social, biological and psychological branches of Gerontology many of the bio-socio-psychological problems of aging of the superannuated and elderly respondents under present study have been assessed.

Geriatric Problems—Physical Help

The superannuated and elderly persons after 60 years of age generally develop some sort of biological trouble and they need a sort of physical help sometimes. It so happens that in certain cases in the beginning of superannuated age of 60 years for some time no geriatric problem is reported. In the present study at an earlier age group; of 60 to 70 years about 62 (26%) respondents do not complain about any geriatric problem. These respondents are distributed as 12(29%), 5(13%),

Table 6.1 : Requiring Physical Help for Geriatric Problem

Requiring Physical Help	*Superannuated University Teachers*		*Superannuated Civil Servants*		*Elderly Lawyers*		*Elderly Doctors*		*Total*	
	f	*%*	*f*	*%*	*f*	*%*	*f*	*%*	*f*	*%*
No Geriatric Problem hence no help required	12	29	05	13	30	25	15	38	62	26
Seeing	25	60	28	70	60	50	20	53	133	56
Hearing	–	–	01	02	06	04	01	03	08	03
Eating	–	–	02	05	08	07	01	03	11	05
Walking (inside the house)	03	07	02	05	08	07	–	–	13	05
Walking (out side the house)	02	04 100	02	05 100	08	07 100	01	03 100	13	05
Total	42	18	40	17	120	50	38	15	240	100

Table 6.2 : Instrumental Help Needed for Geriatric Problem

Instrumental help needed	*Superannuated University Teachers*		*Superannuated Civil Servants*		*Elderly Lawyers*		*Elderly Doctors*		*Total*	
	f	*%*	*f*	*%*	*f*	*%*	*f*	*%*	*f*	*%*
Glasses	25	60	28	70	60	50	20	52	133	55
Hearing machine	–	–	01	03	06	05	01	03	08	03
Walking stick	03	07	02	05	08	07	01	03	14	06
Denture	02	04	02	05	08	07	01	03	13	05
Wheel Chair	–	–	02	05	04	03	–	–	06	03
Foot wear	–	–	–	–	04	03	–	–	04	02
No Instrumental Aid needed	12	29 100	05	12 100	30	25 100	15	39 100	62	26
Total	42	18	40	17	120	50	38	15	240	100/ 100

30(25%) and 15(38%) respectively among the different categories of respondents, i.e. superannuated university teachers, civil servants, elderly lawyers and doctors in Table 6.1 Another important fact is that the most dominant geriatric trouble is with eye, i.e. seeing as reported by 133(56%) respondents on the whole. The distribution of eye trouble among the different categories of respondents is as: 25(60%), 28(70%), 60(50%) and 20(53%) respectively for superannuated university teachers, civil servants, elderly lawyers and doctors. The distribution of other geriatric troubles are as: 8(3%), 11(5%), 13(5%) and 13(5%) respectively for hearing, eating, walking inside the house and walking outside the house.

The distribution as per categorywise respondents is as: 3(7%), and 2(5%) respectively for walking inside and outside the house among, the superannuated university teachers, as 1(2%), 2(5%), 2(5%) and 2(5%) respectively for hearing, eating, walking inside and outside the house among the civil servants; as: 6(4%), 8(7%), 8(7%) and 8(7%) respectively for hearing, eating and walking inside and outside the house among the elderly lawyers; as 1(3%), 1(3%) and 1(3%) respectively for hearing, eating and walking outside the house among the elderly doctors.

Instrumental Help Required

In order to redeem the geriatric problems due to physical aging the elderly and the superannuated persons need use of various instruments for the proper functioning of the physical organs like glasses for eye, hearing machine for ear trouble, the use of denture for eating, wheel chair and footwear for walking inside and outside the house.

In Table 6.2 there are 62(26%) respondents who do not require any help of the above instruments for proper functioning of their main physical organs of the body. They are distributed as : 12(29%), 5(12%), 30(25%) and 15 (39%) respectively among superannuated university teachers, civil servants, elderly lawyers and doctors.

Those taking help of some or the other instrument are distributed on the whole in Table 6.2 as: 133(55%), 8(03%), 14(6%), 13(5%), 6(3%), and 4(2%) respectively for glasses, hearing machine, walking stick, denture, wheel chair and footwear. As per categorywise respondents the distribution is as: 25(60%), 3(7%), 2(4%) respectively for glasses, walking stick and denture among the superannuated university teachers, as 28(7%), 1(3%), 2(5%), 2(5%) and 2(5%) respectively for glasses, hearing machine, walking stick, denture, and wheel chair among the superannuated civil servants; as: 60(50%), 6(5%), 8(7%), 8(7%), 4(3%), and 4(3%) respectively fur glasses, hearing machine, walking stick, denture, wheel chair and footwear among the elderly lawyers; as: 20(52%), 1(3%), 1(3%), and 1(3%) respectively for glasses, hearing machine, walking stick, and denture among the elderly doctors.

Instruments Managed by Whom

In the previous table 6.1 we find 178(74%), respondents using some or the other instrument for their physical upkeep. Now the question arises how do they manage them? In this respect in table 6.3 the distribution of the various sources on the whole is as: 112(47%), 24(10%), 8(3%), 22(9%), and 12(5%) respectively as self, own children/grandchildren, Donors, Governmental and Non-Governmental agency.

Table 6.3 : Instrumental AID Managed by Whom

Instrumental aid managed by	*Superannuated University Teachers*		*Superannuated Civil Servants*		*Elderly Lawyers*		*Elderly Doctors*		*Total*	
	f	*%*	*f*	*%*	*f*	*%*	*f*	*%*	*f*	*%*
Self	25	60	10	25	54	45	23	61	112	47
Own children/ grand children	05	12	09	23	10	08	–	–	24	10
Donors	–	–	–	–	08	07	–	–	08	03
Governmental agency	–	–	16	40	06	05	–	–	22	09
Non-governmental agency	–	–	–	–	12	10	–	–	12	05
Instrumental aid not needed	12	28 100	05	12 100	30	25 100	15	39	62	26
Total	42	18	40	17	120	50	38	15	240	100/ 100

The distribution per categorywise respondents is as: 25(60%), and 5(12%) respectively as Self, own children/grandchildren among the superannuated university teachers; as:10(25%), 9(23%), 16(10%) respectively as Self own, children/grandchildren and governmental agency among the superannuated civil servants; as: 54(45%), 10(8%), 8(7%), 6(5%) and 12(10%) respectively as Self, own children/grandchildren, donors, governmental and non-governmental agency among the elderly lawyers, as: 23(61%), Self alone among the elderly doctors.

General Health and Ailments

Physical aging generally affects the general health of the respondents. Various sorts of illness, debility and disability may crop up in the old age. In this connection as per reporting from the respondents on the whole in Table 6.4 we find as: 62(26%), 45(19%), 118(49%), and

Table 6.4 : General Health and Ailments

General Health Ailments	*Superannuated University Teachers*		*Superannuated Civil Servants*		*Elderly Lawyers*		*Elderly Doctors*		*Total*	
	f	%	*f*	%	*f*	%	*f*	%	*f*	%
On the whole good	12	28	05	12	30	25	15	39	62	26
Minor Illness	10	24	12	31	20	17	03	08	45	19
General Debility	20	48	18	45	60	50	20	53	118	49
Physical	–	–	05	12	10	08	–	–	15	06
Disability				100		100		100		
Total	42	18	40	17	120	50	38	15	240	100/ 100

Table 6.5 : Diseases Respondents Suffer from

Disease	*Superannuated University Teachers*		*Superannuated Civil Servants*		*Elderly Lawyers*		*Elderly Doctors*		*Total*	
	f	%	*f*	%	*f*	%	*f*	%	*f*	%
ENT Trouble	02	05	04	10	05	04	10	26	21	09
Arthrite	07	17	03	08	20	17	–	–	30	12
Asthma	–	–	05	12	09	08	–	–	14	06
Cardiac Problem	12	29	10	25	30	25	–	–	52	21
Blood Pressure	05	12	05	12	05	04	03	08	18	07
Diabetes	03	07	03	08	05	04	10	26	21	09
Skin Disease	–	–	02	05	–	–	–	–	02	01
Psychiatric Problem	–	–	–	–	05	04	–	–	05	02
Stone	–	–	01	03	05	04	–	–	06	03
Prostrate Gland	–	–	02	05	04	01	–	–	06	03
Any other	01	02	–	–	02	02	–	–	03	02
No Disease at All	12	20	05	12	30	25	15	40	62	25
		100		100		100		100		
Total	42	18	40	17	120	50	38	15	240	100/ 100

15(6%) respectively for health on the whole good, minor illness, *General debility and Physical disability.* As per categorywise respondents the distribution is as: 12(28%), 10(24%) and 20(48%) respectively for the health on the whole good, minor illness, and general debility among the superannuated university teachers; as: 5(12%), 12(31%), 18(45%) and 5(12%) respectively for the health on the whole good, minor illness, general debility and physical disability among the superannuated civil servants; as 30(20%), 20(17%),

60(50%), and 10(8%) respectively for the health on the whole good, minor illness, general debility and physical disability among the elderly lawyers; as: 15(39%), 3(8%), 20(53%) respectively for the health on the whole good, minor illness and general debility among the elderly doctors.

Diseases of the Respondents

Although there are 62 (25%) respondents of pretty old age but enjoying normal health. It is only with 178 respondents we have come to know about their diseases. The distribution of which in Table 6.5 is as: 21(9%), 30(12%), 14(6%), 52(21%), 18(7%), 21(9%), 02(1%), 5(2%), 6(3%), 6(3%), and 3(2%) respectively for ENT trouble, arthritis, asthama, cardiac problem, B.P., Dibetis, skin disease, psychiatric problem, stone, prostrate gland and others.

The distribution of different diseases among the different category of respondents is as: 2(5%), 7(17%), 12(29%), 5(12%), 3(7%), and 1(2%) respectively for ENT trouble, arthiritis, cardiac problem, B.P., Diabetis, and other among the superannuated university teachers; as: 4(10%), 3(8%), 5(12%), 10(25%), 5(12 %), 3(8%), 2(5%), 1(3%), and 2(5%) respectively for ENT trouble. arthiritis, asthama, cardiac problem, B.P., Dibetis, skin disease, stone and prostrate gland among the superannuated university teachers; as 5 (4%), 20(17%), 9(8%), 30(25%), 5(4%), 5(4%), 5(4%), 5(4%), 4(3%), and 02(2%) respectively for ENT, trouble, arthritis, asthama, cardiac problem, B.P., Dibetis, skin disease, stone, prostrate gland among the superannuated civil servants; as: 5(4%), 20(17%), 9(8%), 30(25%), 5(4%), 5(4%), 5(4%), 5(4%), 4(3%) and 2(2%) respectively for ENT trouble, Arithritis, Asthama, Cardiac problem, B.P., Diabetis, Psychiatric problem, Stone, Prostrate gland and others among the elderly lawyers; as: 10(26%), 3(8%) and 10(26%) suffer from ENT trouble, B.P. and Diabetis among the elderly doctors.

Type of Treatment Preferred

The popular types of treatment of diseases are chiefly Allopathic, Homeopathic, Ayurvedic, Yunani, Nature cure etc. when asked for their respective preference of a specific type of treatment, if ill, a good number of respondents, i.e. 47(20%) report no opinion about their specific preference.

The different types of treatment as preferred by the respondents are in Table 6.6 as: 80(33%), 44(18%), 36(15%), 05(2%), and 28(12%), respectively for Allopathic, Homeopathic, Ayurvedic, Yunani, Nature cure.

Table 6.6 : Prefering Type of Treatment of Disease by the Respondents

Prefering type of Treatment	*Superannuated University Teachers*		*Superannuated Civil Servants*		*Elderly Lawyers*		*Elderly Doctors*		*Total*	
	f	*%*	*f*	*%*	*f*	*%*	*f*	*%*	*f*	*%*
Allopathic	12	28	10	25	20	17	38	100	80	33
Homeopathic	10	24	09	22	25	21	–	–	44	18
Ayurvedic	04	10	07	17	25	21	–	–	36	15
Yunani	–	–	05	13	–	–	–	–	05	02
Nature Cure	04	10	04	10	20	17	–	–	28	12
No opinion	12	28	05	13	30	24	–	–	47	20
		100		100		100		100		
Total	42	18	40	17	120	50	38	15	240	100/ 100

As per categorywise respondents the distribution is as; 12(28%), 10(24%), 4(10%) and 4(10%) respectively for Allopathic, Homeopathic, Ayurvedic, Nature cure among the superannuated university teachers, as: 10(25%), 9(22%). 7(17%), 5(13%) and 4(10%) respectively for Allopathic, Homeopathic, Ayurvedic, Yunani, Nature cure among the superannuated civil servants, as: 20(17%), 25(21%), 25(21%) and 20(17%) respectively for Allopathic, Homeopathic, Ayurvedic and Nature cure among the elderly lawyers; as: 38(100%) for Allopathic type of treatment among the elderly doctors.

Avoid Consulting a Doctor, if Ill

It is very likely that as a consequence of aging problem some of the ailing respondents avoid consulting a doctor and for which many reasons have been stated by the respondents in Table 6.7 as 39(19%), 18(9%), 11(6%), 116(57%) and 18(9%) respectively for lack of finance, none to bring a doctor nor to take him/her to the doctor, Doctor far-away. No faith on doctor and faith in Nature cure. The categorywise respondents report as: 5(12%); 5(12%), 5(12%), 20(48%) and 7(16%) respectively for lack of finance, none to bring a doctor/nor to take him/her to the doctor, Doctor far away, No faith on doctor, and faith

Table 6.7 : Avoid Consulting A Doctor if Ill

Reasons	*Superannuated University Teachers*		*Superannuated Civil Servants*		*Elderly Lawyers*		*Total*	
	f	*%*	*f*	*%*	*f*	*%*	*f*	*%*
Lack of Finance	05	12	04	10	30	25	39	19
None to bring Doctor Nor take him to the Doctor	05	12	03	07	10	08	18	09
Doctor Far Away	05	12	06	15	–	–	11	06
No Faith on Doctor	20	48	21	53	75	63	116	57
Nature Cure	07	16	06	15	05	04	18	09
		100		100		100		
Total	42	21	40	20	120	59	202	100/ 100

in Nature cure among the superannuated university teachers; as: 4(10%), 3(7%), 6(15%), 21(53%), and 6(15%) respectively for lack of finance, none to bring a doctor/nor to take him/her to the doctor, Doctor far-away, No faith on doctor, faith in nature cure among the superannuated civil servants; as: 30(25%), 10(08%), 75(63%), and 5(4%) respectively for lack of finance, none to bring a doctor/nor to take him/her to the doctor, no faith on doctor, and very much faith in nature cure among the elderly lawyers.

Financing Medical Treatment

The lack of finance in the preceding table is the potent reason for compelling the ailing respondents to avoid consultation with a doctor. Hence the financing for medical treatment in old age is an important issue. In this respect we find the distribution of financial sources for treatment as: 113(47%), 55(23%), 40(17%) and 32(13%) respectively for self, own children/grandchildren, governmental and non-governmental agency in Table 6.8.

The distribution of financial source per categorywise respondents is as: 30(71%), 10(24 %), and 2(5%) respectively for self own children/ grandchildren and Non-Governmental agency among the superannuated university teachers , as: 5(12%), 10(25%), and 25(63%) respectively for self, own children/grandchildren and governmental agency among the superannuated civil servants; as: 40(33%), 35(29%), 15(13%), and 30(25%) respectively for self; own children/grand-children, governmental and non-governmental agency among the elderly lawyers; as: 38(100%) for self among the elderly doctors.

Table 6.8 : Financing Medical Treatment

Financing Medical Treatment	*Superannuated University Teachers*		*Superannuated Civil Servants*		*Elderly Lawyers*		*Elderly Doctors*		*Total*	
	f	*%*	*f*	*%*	*f*	*%*	*f*	*%*	*f*	*%*
Self	30	71	05	12	40	33	38	100	113	47
Own children/ Grandchildren	10	24	10	25	35	29	–	–	55	23
Governmental Agency	–	–	25	63	15	13	–	–	40	17
Non-Governmental Agency	02	05/ 100	–	–/ 100	30	25/ 100	–	–/ 100	32	13
Total	42	18	40	17	120	50	38	15	240	100/ 100

Table 6.9 : Hours of Sleep

Hours of Sleep	*Superannuated University Teachers*		*Superannuated Civil Servants*		*Elderly Lawyers*		*Elderly Doctors*		*Total*	
	f	*%*	*f*	*%*	*f*	*%*	*f*	*%*	*f*	*%*
Upto 6 hrs.	07	17	12	30	40	33	03	08	62	26
6 hrs-8 hrs.	25	60	20	50	60	50	25	66	130	54
More than 8 hrs.	10	23/ 100	08	20/ 100	20	17/ 100	10	26/ 100	48	20
Total	42	18	40	17	120	50	38	15	240	100/ 100

Hours of Sleep

Normally eight hours sound sleep is considered conducive to health. In old age it is seen that the hours of sleep are generally reduced but some of the superannuated and elderly persons still enjoy the past duration of hours of sleep till now. In this connection we find 62(26%), 130(54%), and 48(20%) respondents respectively report upto 6 hrs, 6-8 hrs and more than 8 hrs. As per categorywise respondents this distribution is as: 7(17%), 25(80%), and 10(23%) respectively for upto 6 his, 6 to 8 hrs and more than 8 hrs among the superannuated university teachers; as: 12(3%), 20(50%), and 8(20%) respectively for upto 6 hrs, 6 to 8 hrs and more than 8 hrs among the superannuated civil servants; as: 40(33%), 60(50%) and 20(17%), respectively for upto 6 hrs, 6 to 8 hrs and more than 8 hrs among the elderly lawyers; as: 3(8%), 25(66%) and 10(26%) respectively for upto 6 hrs 6 to 8 hrs and more than 8 hrs among the elderly doctors.

Table 6.10 : Appetite of the Respondents

Appetite	*Superannuated University Teachers*		*Superannuated Civil Servants*		*Elderly Lawyers*		*Elderly Doctors*		*Total*	
	f	*%*	*f*	*%*	*f*	*%*	*f*	*%*	*f*	*%*
Very good	10	24	08	20	10	08	08	21	36	15
Good	25	59	24	60	60	50	25	66	134	56
Fair	05	12	05	12	30	25	05	13	45	19
Neither good nor Fair	02	05/ 100	03	08/ 100	20	17/ 100	–	– 100	25	10
Total	42	18	40	17	120	50	38	15	240	100/ 100

Appetite

Further there is an impact of physical aging on the appetite of the elderly, either it is reduced or menu of meals and other eatables change. While assessing the condition of appetite of the respondents on the whole in Table 6.10 we find its distribution as 36 (15%), 134(56%), 45(19%) and 25(10%) respectively for very good, good, fair and neither good nor fair. As per categorywise respondents the distribution is as: 10(24%), 25(59%), 05(12%), 02(5%) respectively for very good, good, fair and neither good nor fair among the superannuated university teachers, as: 8(20%), 24(60%), 05(12%), and 3(8%) respectively for very good, good, fair and neither good nor fair among the superannuated civil servants; as: 10(8%), 60(50%), 30(25%) and 20(17%) respectively for very good. good, fair and neither good nor fair among the elderly lawyers; as: 8(21%), 25(66%) and 5(13%) respectively for very good, good, fair among the elderly doctors.

Meals Cooked by whom

In old age as a result of aging problem there appears the need for someone's help in cooking the daily meals. Besides spouse, there are son/s, daughter/s, daughter-in-law/s, servants in the family cooking the meals for the elderly and superannuated persons. In this respect on the whole we find the distribution of the persons cooking the meals for the respondents as: 28(12%), 125(52%), 70(29%), 12(5%) and 5(2%) respectively for servant, spouse, son/s, daughter/s and daughter in law/s.

The distribution of the cook as per categorywise respondents in Table 6.11 is as: 8(19%), 20(48%) and 14(33%) respectively for servant, spouse, and son/s; among the superannuated university teachers; as: 25(63%), 13(32%), and 02(5%) respectively for spouse, son/s, and daughter/s among the superannuated civil servants; as: 5(4%), 60(50%), 40(34%), 10(8%) and 5(4%) respectively for servant, spouse, son/s, daughter/s and daughter in law/s among the elderly lawyers; as: 15(39%), 20(53%), and 03(8%) respectively for servant, spouse and son/s among the elderly doctors.

Table 6.11 : Meal Cooked by Whom

Cooked by Whom	*Superannuated University Teachers*		*Superannuated Civil Servants*		*Elderly Lawyers*		*Elderly Doctors*		*Total*	
	f	*%*	*f*	*%*	*f*	*%*	*f*	*%*	*f*	*%*
Servant	08	19	–	–	05	04	15	39	28	12
Spouse/Self	20	48	25	63	60	50	20	53	125	52
Son/s	14	33	13	32	40	34	03	08	70	29
Daughter/s	–	–	02	05	10	08	–	–	12	05
Daughter in law/s	–	–	–	–	05	04	–	–	05	02
		100		100		100		100		
Total	42	18	40	17	120	50	38	15	240	100/ 100

Types of Meal

Generally the elderly due to aging prefer simple meal of easily digestible nature free from cholostrol. Some prefer boiled food stuff only. We can say that the elderly prefer generally vegetarian meal in order to keep themselves fit. There are some having no control on their taste they report mixed nature of meals i.e. both vegetarian and non-vegetarian. In this respect on the whole we find the distribution in Table 6.12 as: 108(45%), 64(27%), and 68(28%) respectively for pure vegetarian, pure non-vegetarian and mixed-vegetarian and non-vegetarian. As per categorywise respondents this distribution is as: 20(48%), 10(24%) and 12(28%) pure vegetarian, pure non-vegetarian and mixed-vegetarian and non-vegetarian among the superannuated university teachers, as: 18(45%), 6(15%), and 16(40%) pure

Table 6.12 : Type of Meals

Type of Meals	*Superannuated University Teachers*		*Superannuated Civil Servants*		*Elderly Lawyers*		*Elderly Doctors*		*Total*	
	f	*%*	*f*	*%*	*f*	*%*	*f*	*%*	*f*	*%*
Pure Vegetarian	20	48	18	45	50	42	20	53	108	45
Pure Non-Vegetarian	10	24	06	15	40	33	08	21	64	27
Mixed-Vegetarian & Non-Vegetarian	12	28/ 100	16	40/ 100	30	25/ 100	10	26/ 100	68	28
Total	42	18	40	17	120	50	38	15	240	100/ 100

vegetarian, pure non-vegetarian and mixedvegetarian and non-vegetarian among the superannuated civil servants; as: 50(42%), 40(33%), and 30(25%) respectively for pure-vegetarian, pure non-vegetarian and mixed-vegetarian and non-vegetarian among the elderly lawyers as: 20(53%), 8(21%), and 10(26%) respectively for pure vegetarian, pure non-vegetarian and mixed-vegetarian and non-vegetarian among the elderly doctors.

Table 6.13 : Meals when and with Whom

Meals when and with Whom	*Superannuated University Teachers*		*Superannuated Civil Servants*		*Elderly Lawyers*		*Elderly Doctors*		*Total*	
	f	*%*	*f*	*%*	*f*	*%*	*f*	*%*	*f*	*%*
Alone First	20	48	15	37	60	50	–	–	95	40
With Spouse	10	24	05	13	10	08	08	21	33	14
With Children/ Grandchildren	10	24	10	25	20	17	25	66	65	27
Alone Last	02	04/ 100	10	25/ 100	30	25/ 100	05	13/ 100	47	19
Total	42	18	40	17	120	50	38	15	240	100/ 100

Meal When and with Whom

Generally the elderly develop habit of taking meals at fixed hours both the times. They also become selective about the person with whom only and the hour they would like to have their meals. In this respect on the whole their choices are distributed in Table 6.13 as: 95(40%), 33(14%), 65(27%), and 47(19%) respectively for Alone first, with spouse, with children/grandchildren and alone last. Such a distribution as per categorywise respondents is as: 20(48%), 10(24%), 10(24%), and 2(4%) respectively for alone first, with spouse, with children/grandchildren and alone last among the superannuated University teachers; as: 15(37%), 5(13%), 10(25%) and 10(25%) respectively for alone first, with spouse, with children/grandchildren and Alone last, among the superannuated civil servants; as: 60(50%), 10(8%), 20(17%) and 30(25%) respectively for Alone first, with spouse, with children/grandchildren and alone last, among the elderly lawyers; as: 8(21%), 25(66%), and 5(13%) respectively for with spouse, with children/grandchildren and alone last, among the elderly doctors.

Reasons for Thinking Self as Unwanted and Worthless

Due to certain reasons the psychology of the elderly is so much affected that they begin to think about himself, as unwanted and worthless creature on earth. Such an extreme pessimistic attitude is an indication of aging problem on the emotional plane. The distribution of reasons for such a thinking about themselves by the respondents on the whole in Table 6.14 is as: 14(6%), 64(27%), 11(05%) and 6(2%) respectively

Table 6.14 : Reasons for Considering Self : As Unwanted and Worthless

Reasons for Thinking self unwanted and worthless	*Superannuated University Teachers*		*Superannuated Civil Servants*		*Elderly Lawyers*		*Elderly Doctors*		*Total*	
	f	*%*	*f*	*%*	*f*	*%*	*f*	*%*	*f*	*%*
No such feeling	29	69	26	65	55	46	35	92	145	60
Discontinuity of work/job/profession	05	12	09	22	–	–	–	–	14	06
Contemptuous attitude of family members	08	19	03	07	50	42	03	08	64	27
No help of economic support from any source	–	–	01	03	10	08	–	–	11	05
Loss of Identity: Social and Professional status and power	–	– 100	01	03 100	05	04 100	–	– 100	06	02
Total	42	18	40	17	120	50	38	15	240	100/100

for reasons of discontinuity of work/jobs/profession, contemptuous attitude of family members, no hope of economic support from any source, loss of identity i.e. social and professional status and power.

As per categorywise respondents we find as : 5(12%), and 8(19%) respectively for reasons of discontinuity of work/ job/ profession and contemptuous attitude of family members among the superannuated university teachers; as: 9(22%), 3(7%), 1(3%) and 1(3%) respectively for reasons of discontinuity of work/job/profession, contemptuous attitude of family members, no hope of economic support from any source, loss of identity, i.e. social and professional status and power among the superannuated civil servants: as: 90(42%), 10(8%), and 9(4%) respectively for contemptuous attitude of family members. No hope of economic support from any source, loss of identity, i.e. social and professional status and power among the elderly lawyers; as: 3(8%), for contemptuous attitude of family members, among the elderly doctors.

Regular Worship and Performing Religious Rites Before and After Superannuation/60 years of Age

It is generally assumed that those elderly having religious faith and performing religious rites regularly are capable of postponing their early aging and lessen the pinch of aging problems.

One of the important hypothesis of this study is that those elderly respondents who have been continuously retaining religious faith and practising religious rites etc. regularly since long before superannuation and 60 years of age and still persisting the same even after superannuation and 60 years of age, are tied with the religious bond which helps them in arresting and deferring early aging and fully equips them well in facing the aging problems very smoothly. With this view we have tried to assess the extent of religious faith and the habit of performing religious activities regularly among the elderly respondents before and after superannuation or 60 years of age.

In this respect in Table 6.15 we find the distribution of religious faith and practice among the respondents before and after superannuation and 60 years of age as 20(48%) before and 30(71%) after, 10(24%) before and (nil) after; 5(12%) before and 2(5%) after, respectively as regularly, often and sometimes among the superannuated university teachers; as 15(38%) before and 28(70%)

Table 6.15 : Regular Worship and Performing Religious Rites Before and after Superannuation/60 Years of Age

Nature of Performing worship and religious activity	*Superannuated university teachers*				*Superannuated Civil Servants*				*Elderly Lawyers*				*Elderly Doctors*			
	Before		*After*		*Before*		*After*		*Before*		*After*		*Before*		*After*	
	f	%	*f*	%	*f*	%	*f*	%	*f*	%	*f*	%	*f*	%	*f*	%
Regularly	20	48	30	71	15	38	28	70	40	33	85	71	05	13	11	29
Often	10	24	–	–	10	25	–	–	40	33	–	–	12	32	–	–
Sometimes	05	12	02	05	12	30	06	15	25	21	10	08	12	32	15	39
Never performing worship and religious activity	07	16/ 100	10	24/ 100	03	07/ 100	06	15/ 100	15	13/ 100	25	21/ 100	09	23/ 100	12	32/ 100
Total	42		42		40		40		120		120		38		38	

after; 10(25%) before and (nil) after, 12(30%) before and 6(15%) after, respectively as regularly, often and sometimes among the superannuated civil servants; as: 40(33%) before, and 85(71%) after, 40(33%) before (nil) after, 25(21%) before and 10(8%) after, respectively as regularly, often and sometimes among the elderly lawyers; as: 5(13%) before and 11(29%) after, 12(32%) and (nil) after, 12(32%) and 15(39%) after respectively for regularly, often and sometimes among the elderly doctors.

Here we find continuous increase in the percentage of the elderly respondents regularly performing religious activities from the past and even after superannuation and 60 years of age to the extent of 23%, 32%, 38% and 16% respectively among the university teachers, civil servants, elderly lawyers and doctors. There is a popular belief that one becomes religious minded in old age, but strange enough there are such cases also who have never performed any religious activity nor having any religious faith from before and still now. The continuous increase in their number after superannuation or 60 years of age is only 8% uniformly among the superannuated university teachers, civil servants, elderly lawyers and doctors refutes the above mentioned popular belief that one becomes religious in old age is confirmed to some extent as there is an increasing number of those becoming religious minded more after superannuation or 60 years of age.

Religious Activities

There are 190 respondents of all the categories who have faith in the Almighty. They perform many forms of religious activities confirming their religious faith. There are 50 respondents of all the categories who do not perform any religious activity. They do so because of having no time for the same or do not believe in performing such activities but showing their interest and faith in God. They are distributed as 10(24%), 6(15%), 25(21%) and 9(24%) respectively among superannuated university teachers, civil servants, elderly lawyers and doctors.

In Table 6.16 the distribution of the various religious activities in order of priority among different categories of respondents is as: 25(60%), 25(60%), 15(42%), 10(24%), 10(24%), 5(12%), and 5(12%) respectively for regular visit to a holy place and worship in the house, Recitation of holy mantras and religious books regularly, Attending

Table 6.16 : Religious Activities

Religious Activities	*Superannuated University Teachers*		*Superannuated Civil Servants*		*Elderly Lawyers*		*Elderly Doctors*	
	f	*%*	*f*	*%*	*f*	*%*	*f*	*%*
Regular visit to a Holy place and daily/often worship in the house	25	60	10	25	50	42	05	13
Attending Religious Discourses	15	42	09	23	50	42	02	05
Arranging religious functions in the house	10	24	06	15	25	21	02	05
Visiting Pilgrim places	10	24	04	10	20	17	04	10
Recitation of Holy mantras & Religious books regularly	25	60	25	63	80	67	05	13
Observing meditation and yogasan etc.	05	12	10	25	35	29	04	10
Observing Jap, Tap, Vrat	05	12	15	38	30	25	05	13
No Religious Activity	10	24	06	15	25	21	09	24
	N-42		N-40		N-120		N-38	

religious discourses, Arranging religious functions in home, Visiting pilgrim places, Observing meditation and yogasan and Observing *Jap, Tap* and *Vrat* among the superannuated university teachers; as: 25(63%), Recitation of holy mantras and religious books regularly, 15(38%). Observing *Jap, Tap* and *Vart,* 10(25%). Regular visit to a holy place and worship in the house, 10(25%) Observing meditation and yogasan, 9(23%) Attending religious discourses, 6(15%) Visiting pilgrim places among the superannuated civil servants, as Recitation of holy *mantras* and religious books regularly 80 (67%), Regular visit to a holy place and worship in the house 50(42%), Attending religious discourses 50(42%), Observing meditation and Yogasan 35(29%), Observing Jap, Tap, Vrat 30(25%), Arranging religious function in home 25(21%), and Visiting pilgrim places by 20(17%), among the elderly lawyers; as Regular visit to a holy place and worship in the house by 5(13%), Recitation of holy *mantras* and religious books regularly by 5(13%), Observing *Jap, Tap* and *Vrat* by 5(13%), Observing meditation and yogasan by 4(10%), Visiting pilgrim places by 4(10%), Observing meditation and yogasan by 4(10%), Attending religious discourses by 2(5%) and Arranging religious function in home by 2(5%) among the elderly doctors.

Gods Blessings

It is generally held that God-blesses his worshipper. In return of various religious activities, faith and concern of the respondents they receive God's blessings in various forms. The distribution of which is reported in descending order in Table 6.17 as Contentment by 30(71%), Tie with community bond by 30(71%), No emotional problem by 30(71%), Feeling completely secured and protected by 30(71%), Normal health by 25(60%), Sweet and amiable relations with all by 25(60%), No liability left unfulfilled by 20(48%), No worry and misery by 15(36%), enjoying social prestige by 10(24%), No deprivation of any sort by 10(24%) among the superannuated university teachers; as: completely secured and protected by 28(70%), Sweet and amiable relations with all by 25(63%), Normal Health by 22(55%), Tie with community bond by 20(50%), Enjoying social prestige by 15(47%), Contentment by 15(47%), No emotional problem by 15(47%), No worry and misery by 10(25%), No liability left unfulfilled by 10(25%) and No deprivation of any sort by 5(12%) among the superannuated civil servants; as: Tie with community bond by 100(83%), completely secured and protected by 100(83%), Contentment by 90(75%), Normal health by 80(67%), Sweet and amiable relations with all by 75(63%);

Table 6.17 : God's Blessings in the form of Desire Fulfilment and the Desired Achievements

God's blessings desire fulfilment and desired achievements	*Superannuated University Teachers*		*Superannuated Civil Servants*		*Elderly Lawyers*		*Elderly Doctors*	
	f	*%*	*f*	*%*	*f*	*%*	*f*	*%*
Normal Health	25	60	22	55	80	67	15	39
No Worry and Misery	15	36	10	25	50	42	15	39
Enjoying Social Prestige	10	24	15	47	50	42	15	39
Contentment	30	71	15	47	90	75	15	39
Tie with Community Bond	30	71	20	50	100	83	15	39
No Emotional Problem	30	71	15	47	60	50	15	39
No Liability	20	48	10	25	50	42	15	39
Completely secured and protected	30	71	28	70	100	83	10	26
Sweet and Amiable relations with All	25	60	25	63	75	63	15	39
No Deprivation of Any sort	10	24	05	12	40	33	10	26
	N-42		N-40		N-120		N-38	

No emotional problem by 60(50%), No worry and misery by 50(42%), Enjoying Social prestige by 50(42%), No liability left unfulfilled by 50(42%), and No deprivation of any sort by 40(33%) among the elderly lawyers; as Normal health 15(39%), No worry and misery 15(39%), Enjoying Social prestige 15(39%), Contentment 15(39%), Tie with community bond 15(39%), No emotional problem 15(39%), No liability lest unfulfilled 15(39%), Sweet and amiable relations with all 15(39%), completely secured and protected 10(26%), No deprivation of any sort 10(26%), among the elderly doctors. All these God's blessings to the worshipper respondents definitely fully equip them not to think of Aging and face all the aging problems if any with full courage and peacefully.

Agreeing with Some Popular Statements

There are many popular statements relating to the aging problems. Some of the most prevalent statements are:

(i) Children main support to the elderly in old age.
(ii) Youngsters have less respect to their elders.
(iii) The elderly more dependent on spouse/sons/daughters in old age.
(iv) One becomes more god fearing and religious in old age.

The respondents either agree or disagree or report no opinion about the statements. In this respect we find distribution of their opinion in Tables 6.18 as: Agree with 30(71%), Disagree with 10(24%) and No opinion 2(5%) about the I Statement; as Agree with 32(76%), Disagree with 8(19%), and no opinion 2(5%) about II statement; As Agree with 30(71%), Disagree with 10(240/°), and No opinion 2(5%), about III statement; as : Agree with 25(60%), Disagree with 10(24%) and No opinion 7(16%), about the statement IV among the superannuated university teachers.

Among the superannuated civil servants the views are as: Agree with 30(75%), and Disagree with 10(25%), for statement I, as: Agree with 35(87%), and disagree with 5(13%) for the statement II; as again Agree with 35(87%) and Disagree with 5(13%) for the statement III; as: Agree with 38(95%) and Disagree with 2(5%) about the statement IV.

Table 6.18 : Opinion about Popular Statements

Popular Statements	*Superannuated Univ. teachers*						*Superannuated Civil Servants*						*Elderly Lawyers*						*Elderly Doctors*					
	Agree		*Dis-Agree*		*No Opinion*		*Agree*		*Dis-Agree*		*No Opinion*		*Agree*		*Dis-Agree*		*No Opinion*		*Agree*		*Dis-Agree*		*No Opinion*	
	f	%	*f*	%	*f*	%	*f*	%	*f*	%	*f*	%	*f*	%	*f*	%	*f*	%	*f*	%	*f*	%	*f*	%
I. Children support to the elderly in old age	30	71	10	24	02	05	30	75	10	25	–	–	100	83	15	12	05	05	08	21	30	79	–	–
II. Youngsters have less respect for the elderly	32	76	08	19	02	05	35	87	05	13	–	–	90	75	20	17	10	08	30	79	08	21	–	–
III. The elderly more depedent on Spouse/ Sons/Daughters in old age	30	71	10	24	02	05	35	87	05	13	–	–	100	83	20	17	–	–	08	21	30	79	–	–
IV. One becomes God Fearing and Religious in old age	25	60	10	24	07	16	38	95	02	05	–	–	115	96	–	–	05	04	30	80	04	10	–	–

Among the elderly lawyers there are 100(835) Agree with, 15(12%) Disagree with, and 5(5%) having no opinion about the statement I, as: 90(75%) Agree with, 20(17%) Disagree with and 10(8%) having no opinion about the statement II; as: 100(83%) agree with and 20(17%) Disagree with the statement III; as 115(96%) Agree with and 5(4%) having no opinion about statement IV.

Among the elderly doctors the respondents Agree with 8(21%), and Disagree 30(79%) with the statement I, Agree with 30(79%) and disagree with 8(21%) about the statement, II, Again Agree with 8(21%) and Disagree with 30(79%), about the statement III; Agree with 30(80%), Disagree with 4(10%) and having no opinion 4(10%) about the statement IV.

Leisure Time Activities

The leisure time activities among the superannuated university teachers are distributed in Table 6.19 on priority basis as Listening to Radio and cassetts and seeing the television by almost all, i.e. 42(100%),

Table 6.19 : Leisure-Time Activities

Leisure Time Activities	*Superannuated University Teachers*		*Superannuated Civil Servants*		*Elderly Lawyers*		*Elderly Doctors*	
	f	*%*	*f*	*%*	*f*	*%*	*f*	*%*
Reading Novels/Magazines/ News Papers/ New Publications/Current Professional Journals	35	83	20	50	60	50	35	92
Listening to Radio/Cassets and Seeing the television	42	100	40	100	115	96	25	66
Writing letters, Articles/ Reports/Preparing Notes/ Composing poems	30	71	05	12	70	58	05	13
Recitation of Holy Books (Regularly)	10	24	35	88	100	83	10	26
Morning & Evening Walk	30	71	35	88	80	67	25	66
Indoor Games	30	71	10	25	15	12	–	–
Gardening	15	36	10	25	10	08	25	66
Attending Club	01	02	–	–	10	08	30	79
Gossip with Friends and Neighbours	03	07	10	25	20	16	05	13
Doing Social Services	04	10	–	–	20	16	12	32
	N-42		N-40		N-120		N-38	

Reading novels, magazines/Newspapers/New Publications/ Current Professional journals by 35(83%), writing letters, Articles, Reports, Preparing Notes and writing poems by 30(71%), Morning and Evening walk by 30(71%), Indoor games by 30(71%), Gardening by 15(36%), Recitation of holy books by 10(24%), Doing social service by 4(10%), Gossip with friends and neighbours by 3(7%) and Attending club by 1(2%).

The distribution among the superannuated civil servants as per their preference is as: Listening to Radio and cassetts and seeing the television by 40(100%), Recitation of holy books by 35(88%), Morning and Evening walk by 35(88%), Reading novels, magazines/ Newspapers/New Publications/Current Professional journals by 20(50%), Indoor games by 10(25%), Gardening by 10(25%), and Gossip with friends and neighbours by 10(25%), Writing letters, Articles, Reports, Preparing Notes and writing poems etc. by 5(12%).

Similarly among the elderly lawyers we find such a distribution on priority basis as: Listening to Radio and cassetts by 115(96%), Recitation of holy books by 100(83%), Morning and Evening walk by 80(67%), writing letters, Articles, Reports, Preparing Notes and writing poems by 70(58%) and Reading Novels/Magazines/ Newspapers/New Publications/Current Professional Journals by 60(50%), Gossip with friends and neighbours by 20(16%), doing social service by 20(16%), Indoor games by 15(12%), Gardening by 10(8%) and Attending Club by 10(8%).

Among the elderly doctors leisure time activities are on priority basis as: Reading Novels/Magazines/News papers/New Publications/ Current Professional Journals by 35(92%), Attending club by 30(79%), Listening to Radio/Cassetts and seeing the television by 25(66%), Morning and evening walk by 25(66%), Gardening by 25(66%), Doing social service by 12(32%), Recitation of holy books by 10(26%), writing letters/ Articles, Reports / Preparing Notes and writing poems by 5(13%) and Gossip with friends and neighbours by 5(13%).

Settling Down at the Native Place with landed Property

Most of the respondents own landed property at their native place but they are not at all inclined to settle down there either because of rural site or many of the urban activities to which they have become addict to. In this respect we find out the entirely a negative response toward settling down at the native place from 177(74%) and positive response only to the extent of 63(26%) in Table 6.20. The response as per categorywise respondents we find positive 20(18%) and Negative 22(52%) responses for settling down at the native place among the superannuated university teachers; as 10(25%) and 30(75%) respectively for positive and negative responses among the elderly lawyers; as 3(8%), and 35(92%) respectively for positive and negative responses among the elderly doctors. This shows that most of the respondents, have lost their attachment with the land or place of their birth and early nurture.

Table 6.20 : Intention of Settling Down at the Native Place

Respondent	*Intention of Settling Down at the Native Place*					
	Yes		*No*		*Total*	
	f	*%*	*f*	*%*	*f*	*%*
Superannuated University Teachers	20	48	22	52	42	17
Superannuated Civil Servants	10	25	30	75	40	17
Elderly Lawyers	30	25	90	75	120	50
Elderly Doctors	03	08/ 100	35	92/ 100	38	16
Total	63	26	177	74	240	

Where and With Whom to Live After Superannuation/60 years of age

As a consequence of aging problem the elderly are compelled to take vital decision about their future stay with whom. In this respect the respondents in Table 6.21 on the whole prefer to stay as: 20(8%) with spouse, 160(67%) with son/s, 24(10%) with daughter/s, 7(03%) with relatives and 29(12%) thinking about joining Old Age Home. Here

Table 6.21 : Where and with whom to live after Superannuation/60 Years of Age

Where and with whom to live after Superannuation or	*Superannuated University Teachers*		*Superannuated Civil Servants*		*Elderly Lawyers*		*Elderly Doctors*		*Total*	
60 years of age	*f*	*%*	*f*	*%*	*f*	*%*	*f*	*%*	*f*	*%*
Spouse	04	10	03	07	10	08	03	08	20	08
Son/s	25	60	30	75	75	62	30	79	160	67
Daughter/s	06	14	05	13	08	07	05	13	24	10
Relative/s	05	11	–	–	02	02	–	–	07	03
Old Age Home	02	05/ 100	02	05/ 100	25	21/ 100	–	– 100	29	12
Total	42		40		120		38		240	100

we find that mostly the respondents like to live with son/s, i.e. 160(67%) and this tendency of prefering to live with their son/s is highly indicated among all the categories of respondents. Further we find 4(10%), 25(60%), 6(14%), 5(11%), and 2(5%) respectively for spouse, son/s, daughter/s, relative/s and Old Age Home among the superannuated university teachers; as: 3(7%), 30(75%), 5(13%), and 2(5%) respectively for spouse, son/s, daughter/s and Old Age Home among the superannuated civil servants; as: 10(8%), 75(62%), 8(7%), 2(2%), 25(21%), respectively for spouse, son/s, daughter/s, relative/s and Old Age Home among the superannuated lawyers; as 3(8%), 30(79%), and 5(13%) respectively for spouse, son/s, daughter/s among the elderly doctors.

Family Reaction if Intend to Join Old Age Home by the Respondents

Although generally the elderly respondents do not like to pass rest of their life in Old Age Home but sometimes under certain compelling situations they may have no option but to join Old Age Home. If they join or intend to join Old Age Home the respondents' family has both affirmative and negative reaction and sometime indecisive. In this respect in Table 6.22 we find on the whole as 25(10%), 198(83%) and 17(7%) respectively as Affirmative, Negative and Indecisive stand.

Table 6.22 : Family Reaction if Intend to Join Old Age Home

Nature of Reaction	*Superannuated University Teachers*		*Superannuated Civil Servants*		*Elderly Lawyers*		*Elderly Doctors*		*Total*	
	f	*%*	*f*	*%*	*f*	*%*	*f*	*%*	*f*	*%*
Affirmative	05	12	–	–	20	16	–	–	25	10
Negative	35	83	35	88	90	76	38	100	198	83
Indecisive	02	05/ 100	05	12/ 100	10	08/ 100	–	– 100	17	07
Total	42	–	40	03	120	–	38	–	240	–

The distribution of reaction of the categorywise respondents' family we find as: 5(12%), 35(83%), and 2(5%) respectively as Affirmative, Negative and Indecisive stand as reported by the superannuated university teachers; as: 35(88%) and 5(12%) respectively as Negative and Indecisive stand as reported by the superannuated civil servants; as: 20(16%), 90(76%), and 10(8%) respectively as Affirmative, Negative and Indecisive stand as reported by the elderly lawyers and all the elderly doctors', i.e. 38(100%) a negative attitude of family members toward joining of Old Age Home. This shows that the majority of respondents' families would not like any of their elderly member joining an Old Age Home. This shows that traditional preference is still effective and favours the elderly's living in his/her own family and it is the responsibility of family members for looking after them in old age.

Reasons for Joining Old Age Home

Even if the respondents wish to join Old Age Home it is only because of two main reasons. There are in all 42 such respondents distributed as 7, 5 and 30 respectively among the superannuated University teachers, Civil servants and the elderly lawyers, wishing to join Old Age Home stating reasons as: 28(7%), and 14(33%) respectively as contemptuous attitude of the family members and wishing to have no obligation from any family member in Table 6.23. As categorywise respondents we find 5(71%) and 2(29%) among the superannuated university teachers, 3(60%), and 2(40%) among the superannuated civil servants, and 20(67%) and 10(33%) among the elderly lawyers respectively for reasons of contemptuous attitude of family members, and wishing to have no obligation from any family member.

Table 6.23 : Reasons for Joining Old Age Home

Consideration for Joining Old Age Home	*Superannuated University Teachers*		*Superannuated Civil Servants*		*Elderly Lawyers*		*Total*	
	f	*%*	*f*	*%*	*f*	*%*	*f*	*%*
Contemptuous attitude of family members	05	71	03	60	20	67	28	67
Wishing to have no obligation from any family member	02	29/ 100	02	40/ 100	10	33/ 100	14	33
Total	07	–	05	–	30	–	42	84

Unpleasant Aspect of Life

The unpleasant aspects are mainly the aging problems with which most of the respondents are affected. Only 30 respondents i.e. 10(24%), and 20(53%) respectively among the superannuated university teachers and elderly doctors do not feel the pinch of any unpleasant aspect. This means they are away from the pinch of aging problems.

On the whole the distribution of unpleasant aspects in Table 6.24 is as: 84(35%), 110(46%), 64(26%), 19(8%), 80(33%), 65(27%), 30(12%), 85(35%), 80(33%), and 88(37%) respectively for Disrespect in family, Away from children/grand children, Loneliness, social alienation, Bad health, Dependency, Unwantedness, None Cares to help nor speaks consolatory words, None cares personal feelings and whims and having no son.

Table 6.24 : Unpleasant Aspect of Life

Unpleasant Aspect of Life	*Superannuated University Teachers*		*Superannuated Civil Servants*		*Elderly Lawyers*		*Elderly Doctors*		*Total*	
	f	*%*	*f*	*%*	*f*	*%*	*f*	*%*	*f*	*%*
Disrespect in the family	10	24	20	50	60	50	04	11	84	35
Away from the Children/Grand-children	20	48	25	62	40	33	25	66	110	46
Loneliness	10	24	15	38	35	29	04	11	64	26
Social Alienation	–	–	04	12	15	13	–	–	19	08
Bad Health	15	36	20	50	45	38	–	–	80	33
Dependency	05	12	20	50	40	33	–	–	65	27
Unwantedness	–	–	05	12	25	21	–	–	30	12
None cares to help Nor speaks consolatory words	05	12	20	50	60	50	–	–	85	35
None cares personal feelings and whims	05	12	25	62	50	42	–	–	80	33
Having No son	10	24	23	57	55	46	–	–	88	37
No Unpleasant Aspect in life	10	24	–	–	–	–	20	53	30	12
	N-42		N-40		N-120		N-38		N-240	

The distribution of the aging problems or unpleasant aspects of life per categorywise respondents among the superannuated university teachers in a descending order is as: 20(48%), 15(36%), 10(24%), 10(24%), 10(24%), 5(12%), 5(12%), and 5(12%), respectively for Away from children/ grand children, Bad health, Disrespect in family, Loneliness, having no son, Dependency, None Cares to help nor speaks consolatory words, None cares personal feelings and whims.

Among the superannuated civil servants the distribution is as: 25(62%), 25(62%), 23(57%). 20(50%), 20(50%), 20(50%), 20(50%), 15(38%), 5(12%), and 4(12%) respectively for Away from children/ grand children, None cares personal feelings and whims, Having no son, Disrespect in family, Bad health, Dependency, None cares to help nor speaks consolatory words, loneliness, unwantedness, and social alienation.

Among the elderly lawyers we find as 60(50%), 60(50%), 55(46%), 50(42%), 45(38%), 40(33°%), 40(33%), 35(29%), 25(21%), and 15(13%) respectively for Disrespect in family, None cares to help nor speaks consolatory words, Having no son, None cares personal feelings and whims, Bad health, Away from children/ grand children, Loneliness, Unwantedness and Social alienation.

Among the elderly doctors 25(66%), 4(11%), and 4(11%) respectively for Away from the children/grand children, Disrespect in family and loneliness.

In this way on the whole the main aging problems felt by the respondents in descending order as Away from the children/grand children, Having No Son, None cares to help nor speaks consolatory words, Disrespect in family, Bad health, None cares personal feelings and whims, Dependency, Loneliness, Unwantedness and Social alienation.

Depression

The most common consequence of physical aging is depression as very often felt by the elderly people due to advancing age, but there are good number of exceptions in the present study. In the present study 183(76%) respondents report no such a feeling of depression; they are categorywise distributed as 40(22%), 25(14%), 80(44%) and 38(20%) respectively among the superannuated university teachers, civil servants, elderly lawyers and doctors. Those 57(24%) respondents reporting depression are distributed as 2(4%), 15(26%) and 40(70%) respectively among the superannuated university teachers, civil servants, elderly lawyers with an exception of elderly doctors respondents.

The distribution as per categorywise respondents of affirmative and negative reporting of depression in Table 6.25 is as: 2(5%) and 40(95%) among the superannuated university teachers, 15(37%) and 25(63%) among the superannuated civil servants, 40(33%) and

80(67%) among the elderly lawyers, one and 38(100%) among the elderly doctors respectively for Yes and No reporting about depression.

Table 6.25 : Whether Feeling Depressed

Whether Feeling Depressed	*Superannuated University Teachers*		*Superannuated Civil Servants*		*Elderly Lawyers*		*Elderly Doctors*		*Total*	
	f	*%*	*f*	*%*	*f*	*%*	*f*	*%*	*f*	*%*
Yes	02	05	15	37	40	33	–	–	57	24
No	40	95	25	63	80	67	38	100	183	76
Total	42	100	40	100	120	100	38	100	240	100

Reasons for feeling Depression

Those 57(24%) respondents reporting depression, have stated certain reasons as declining social cultural values by 6(10%) frequent shift of dwelling place by 14(46%) and bereavement by 11(19%) in Table 6.26.

Table 6.26 : Reasons for Feeling Depressed

Reasons	*Superannuated University Teachers*		*Superannuated Civil Servants*		*Elderly Lawyers*		*Total*	
	f	*%*	*f*	*%*	*f*	*%*	*f*	*%*
Declining Social Cultural Values	02	100	–	–	04	10	06	10
Frequent shift of dwelling place	–	–	05	33	09	23	14	25
Thin Social Relations with others	–	–	06	40	20	50	26	46
Bereavement	–	–	04	27	07	17	11	19
Total	02	100	15	100	40	100	57	100

The distribution of different reasons for depression is as declining social cultural values by 2(10%) superannuated university teachers; as frequent shift of dwelling place by 5(33%), thin social relations with others by 6(4%) and bereavement by 4(27%) among the superannuated civil servants, as declining social and cultural values by 4(10%), frequent shift of dwelling place by 9(23%), thin social relations with others by 20(50%) and bereavement by 7(17%) among the elderly lawyers.

Major Wishes and Desires

The elderly persons have many wishes and desires. They are always anxious about them and expect some one to help them in materialising their wishes and desires. In this respect the younger family members, governmental and non-governmental agencies, medical experts and psychiatrists can be of great help to them.

In Table 6.27 we find distribution of the major wishes and desires of the superannuated university teachers in descending order as : Peaceful and contented life by 42(100%), Normal health by 42(100%), No dependency by 42(100%), No serious illness by 42(100%), Natural/normal death by 42(100%), No liability by 40(95%), Sweet home and Sweet tongue of all by 40(95%), company of the devotees of the same sect by 32(76%), ever enjoying social status and power by 30(76%) and absence of any economic need by 10(24%).

Table 6.27 : Major Wishes and Desires

Wishes and Desires	*Superannuated University Teachers*		*Superannuated Civil Servants*		*Elderly Lawyers*		*Elderly Doctors*		*Total*	
	f	%	*f*	%	*f*	%	*f*	%	*f*	%
Peaceful and contented life	42	100	40	100	120	100	38	100	240	100
Ever Enjoying Social Status and Power	30	76	35	88	90	75	35	92	190	79
Company of the Devotees (the same panth)	32	77	30	75	100	83	10	26	172	72
Normal Health	42	100	40	100	120	100	38	100	240	100
No Dependency	42	100	40	100	120	100	38	100	240	100
Absence of any Economic Need	10	24	35	88	90	75	-	-	135	56
No Liability	40	95	40	100	100	83	38	100	218	91
Sweet home with sweet tongued people	40	95	40	100	100	83	38	100	218	91
No Serious Illness	42	100	40	100	120	100	38	100	240	100
Natural/Normal Death	42	100	40	100	120	100	38	100	240	100
Total	N-42		N-40		N-120		N-38		N/T-240	

Among the superannuated civil servants the distribution in descending order of their wishes and desires is as: Peaceful and Contented life by 40(100%), Normal health by 40(100%), No dependency by 40(100%), No liability by 40(100%), sweet home and sweet tongue of all by 40(100%), No serious illness by 40(100%), Natural and normal death by 40(100%), Ever enjoying social status and power by 35(88%), Absence of any economic need by 35(88%), and company of the devotees of the same sect by 30(75%).

The distribution of wishes and desires among the elderly lawyers is as: Peaceful and Contented life 120(100%), Normal health 120(100%), No dependency 120(100%), No serious illness 120(100%), Natural and normal death 120(100%), Company of the devotees of the same sect 100(83%), No liability 100(83%), sweet home and sweet tongue of all 100(83%), ever enjoying social status and power 90(75%) and absence of any economic need 90(75%).

Similarly among the elderly doctors, we find this distribution as : all of them, i.e. 38(100%), have expressed their major wishes and desires as Peaceful and Contented life, Normal health, No dependency, No liability, Sweet home and Sweet tongue of all, No serious illness. Natural and normal death; 35(92%) and 10(26%) respectively for ever enjoying social status and power and company of the devotees of the same sect.

Bio-socio-psychological Problems

The chief bio-socio-psychological problems on the whole are distributed in Table 6.28 in descending order as physical debility by 180(75%), family tension by 145(60%), Loneliness by 115(48%), economic problem by 110(46%), worries and anxieties by 105(44%), Death phobia by 95(40%), Dependency by 87(36%) and Hallucination by 50(21%).

The distribution of aging problems in descending order is as: 35(83%) for physical debility, 30(71%) for loneliness; 25(60%) for family tension, 15(36%) for worries and anxieties, 10(24%) for economic problem and 10(24%) for death phobia among the superannuated university teachers; as: 35(88%) for physical debility, 35(88%) for worries and anxicties, 32(80%) for dependency, 30(75%) for family tension, 30(75%), for economic problem, 30(75%) for loneliness, 25(63%) for death phobia, and 15(38%) for Hallucination among the superannuated civil servants; as: 100(83%) for physical

Table 6.28 : Main Problems of Aging

Main Problems of Aging	*Superannuated University Teachers*		*Superannuated Civil Servants*		*Elderly Lawyers*		*Elderly Doctors*		*Total*	
	f	%	*f*	%	*f*	%	*f*	%	*f*	%
Physical Debility	35	83	35	88	100	83	10	26	180	75
Family Tension	25	60	30	75	90	75	–	–	145	60
Economic Problem	10	24	30	75	70	58	–	–	110	46
Death Phobia	10	24	25	63	60	50	–	–	95	40
Loneliness	30	71	30	75	50	42	05	13	115	48
Dependency	05	12	32	80	50	42	–	–	87	36
Worries and Anxieties	15	36	35	88	55	46	–	–	105	44
Hallucination	–	–	15	38	35	29	–	–	50	21
Total	N-42		N-40		N-120		N-38		N-240	

debility, 90(75%) for family tension, 70(58%) for economic problem. 60(50%) for Death phobia, 55(46%) for worries and Anxieties, 50(42%) for loneliness, 50(42%) for dependency, 35(29%) Hallucination among the elderly lawyers; as: 10(26%) for physical debility and 5(13%) for loneliness, among the elderly doctors.

Major Expectations from the Government

The elderly respondents facing many sorts of aging problems which can be coped with only by the generous and humanitarian stand of the government. Hence the senior citizens have many sorts of expectations from the government to help them in controlling all sorts of aging problems. These demands from the government on the whole are distributed in descending order as Separate counters at public places for the senior citizens by 237(99%), Subsidy in essential consumption goods and articles by 210(88%), Concessions and rebates etc. in prices of commodities of daily use by 205(85%), Mobile medical facility at home of all the elderly by 202(84%), Separate Geriatric ward in civil hospitals, medical colleges and Health centres by 202(84%), Remunerative engagement of senior citizens utilising their expertise, skill, excellence and long experience by 175(73%), Membership in Government committees and Commissions for the welfare of the elderly by 145(60%); Time bound revision of pension by 82(34%) and Government sponsored/run Old Age Homes / Day Care Centres with all home like facilities by 50(21%).

Table 6.29 : Major Demands from the Government

Major Demands	*Superannuated University Teachers*		*Superannuated Civil Servants*		*Elderly Lawyers*		*Elderly Doctors*		*Total*	
	f	*%*	*f*	*%*	*f*	*%*	*f*	*%*	*f*	*%*
Time Bound Revision of Pension	42	100	40	100	–	–	–	–	82	34
Concession, Rebate and Subsidy in the Prices of Commodities of daily use	30	71	40	100	120	100	15	39	205	85
Membership in Govt. Committees, Commissions for the Welfare of the Elderly	40	95	20	50	50	42	35	92	145	60
Subsidy in Essential consumption goods and articles	40	95	40	100	120	100	10	26	210	88
Separate counters at public places for the senior citizens	42	100	40	100	120	100	35	92	237	99
Remunerative Engagement of Senior Citizens utilizing their expertise, skill, excellence & long experience of work	40	95	20	50	90	75	25	66	175	73
Mobile Medical help at the elderly's residence	42	100	40	100	120	100	–	–	202	84
Separate Geriatric Ward in Civil Hospitals, Medical College and Health Centres	42	100	40	100	120	100	–	–	202	84
Govt. Sponsored Orphanages, Old Age Homes and Day care Centres with all facilities	05	12	10	25	35	29	–	–	50	21
Total	N	42	N	40	N	120	N	38	N	240

The distribution of their expectations from the government is in descending order as: Separate counters at public places for the senior citizens by all, i.e. 42(100%), Mobile medical facility at home of all the elderly by all, 42(100%), again separate Geriatric ward in civil hospital, Medical college and Health Centres by 42(100%), Time bound revision of pension by 42(100%), Concession and rebates etc. in prices of commodities of daily use by 30(71%), and 5(12%) for government sponsored and run Old Age Homes/ Day Care Centres with all the home like facilities among the superannuated university teachers.

40 respondents (100%) each for Time bound revision of pension, Concession and rebates etc. in prices of commodities of all daily use; Subsidy in essential consumption goods and articles, Separate counters at public places for the senior citizens, Mobile medical facility at home of all the elderly and Separate Geriatric ward in civil hospital, Medical College, and Health Centres, 20(50%) for Remunerative engagement of senior citizens utilizing their expertise, skill, excellence and long experience and 10(25%) for government sponsored/run Old Age Homes/ Day Care Centres with all facilities among the superannuated civil servants.

As regards the elderly lawyers we find the distribution of their demands from the government in descending order as 120(100%) for Concession and rebates etc. in prices of commodities and articles of daily use, Subsidy in essential consumption goods and articles; Separate counters at public places for the senior citizens, Mobile medical facility at home of all the elderly and Separate Geriatric ward in civil hospital, Medical College, and Health Centres, 90(75%) for Remunerative engagement of senior citizens utilizing their expertise, skill, excellence and long experience of work, 50(42%) for Membership in Government Committees and Commissions for the welfare of the elderly and 35(29%) for Government sponsored/run Old Age Homes/Day Care Centres with all facilities.

In respect of elderly doctors we find only few of their demands from the government in descending order as 35(92%) for Membership in Government Committees and Commissions for the welfare of the elderly, 35(92%) Separate counters at public places for the senior citizens, 25(66%) for Remunerative engagement of senior citizens utilizing their expertise, skill, excellence and long experience of work, 15(39%) for Concession and rebates etc. in prices of commodities of dally use and 10(26%) for Subsidy in essential consumption goods and articles of daily use.

Conclusion

The bio-psychological problems of aging are geriatric ailments, such as general health and diseases, sleep, appetite and type of meal and treatment efforts etc. and psychological problems like considering self as unwanted, religious faith and God's blessings, views about popular sayings about aging, considering dependable persons and decision about stay with whom and views about joining Old Age Homes etc. Further other related aspects are leisure time activities, unpleasantness, depression, personal wishes and desires and expectations from the government etc.

The main geriatric trouble is reported by the majority, i.e. 133(56%) respondents is eyesight. As regards general health we find a good number 62(26%) reporting the general health on the whole good and 118(49%) reporting general debility as the main physical ailment. The main diseases by which they suffer from are: cardiac problem (Heart disease) by 52(21%), Arthirite, 30(12%) ENT trouble, 21(9%) Blood Pressure 18(7%) and Asthama 14(6%). The most preferred type of treatment is Allopathic by 80(35%). Further on the whole hours of sleep, appetite and type of meal etc. are quite normal and of vegetarian preference. 130(54%) report sleep between 6 to 8 hrs per day, good appetite by 134(58%), and 108(45%), prefer vegetarian meal. One of the important hypothesis related to religious worship as practised in present study is validated. Here we find in Table 6.15 a continuous increase in the percentage of those performing regular worship from before and even after superannuation or 60 years of age to the extent of 23 per cent, 32 per cent, 38 per cent and 16 per cent respectively among the superannuated university teachers, civil servants, elderly lawyers and doctors. These respondents neither ever bother for aging nor they ever need for coping with any aging problem. Hence one of the important hypothesis of this study "those who have been althrough religious minded and maintain this tendency even after superannuation or 60 years of age do not feel the problems of fast aging", is validated.

In Table 6.17 we find respondents tied with social and community bond to the extent of 71 per cent among superannuated university teachers, 50 per cent among superannuated civil servants, 83 per cent among elderly lawyers and 39 per cent among elderly doctors as well as Gods blessings, in the form: Normal health, no worries and miseries, enjoying social prestige, full contentment and feeling completely secured and protected, hence our very first hypothesis based on Emile Durkheim's Viewpoint that *"so long people of any class age, gender and creed are closely knitted with social bond are hale and hearty and feel lesser the pinch of aging in the case of senior citizens"* is also validated.

Further we find more optimistic views of the respondents in Table 6.18. Instead of idling away their increased leisure hours after superannuation or 60 years of age they enjoy it well and engage themselves in useful activities and devote much of their leisure hours also for charitable social service.

We further find that most of the respondents do not like to join Old Age Homes etc. rather prefer their stay in their own family and live among their own family members. The main aging problem is the physical debility as reported by 180(75%) repondents which is very usual with the advancing age of the individuals. The major expectations of the respondents from the Government are timebound revision of pension, income tax relief, priority in house allotment, foodstuffs on controlled price, free medical treatment, mobile dispensary etc.

7 IN LIEU OF CONCLUSION—FINDINGS, DISCUSSION AND SUGGESTIONS

Care of the elderly is a challenge, faced by the societies around the world. As medical advances allow more people to live longer lives, we have to ensure that the seniors enjoy the benefits they deserve in their last years. Average life expectancy in India has increased from 23 years in 1901 as 25 years at the time of independence to 61 years today. More than 43 per cent of all persons in the world aged 75 and older live in just four countries China, and United States (having the largest proportion), followed by India and Japan. The longevity explosion is a triumph and a testament to human problem solving.

Findings and Discussion

This is a sociological study of aging among the four categories of senior citizens (240) distributed as 42 superannuated university teachers, 40 civil servants, 120 Elderly (60+) lawyers and 38 Elderly (60+) doctors. The findings of the present study are based on statistical estimation of the data in 64 tables containing information so received by 240 respondents. The findings relate to the biological psychological, socio-economic and cultural aspects of aging problems and adjustments. Although, as per research design of the present study, i.e. "Exploratory-cum-Descriptive" there is hardly any need of testing a hypothesis but for the sake of a depth analysis and comparative assessment of the aging problems among the four categories of senior citizens through Sociological Perspective the following are the important findings relative to some of the tentative hypotheses as formulated and put to test in the present study.

(i) As per eminent French Sociologist Emile Durkheim's view 'as long as the people of any class, gender, age and creed are closely knitted with social bond, they do not at all feel much the pangs of aging but the moment the senior citizens are away from the social bond they feel socially alienated and begin to experience fast aging which becomes a problem.' This is a Sociological Perspective approach, the main thrust of the present study.

(ii) The retired persons experience fast aging if they are deprived of the continuity to work. On the other hand those senior citizens who remain actively involved in work, job and profession even after superannuation or 60 years of age do not experience fast aging problems.

(iii) One of the important base of social bond in every society is religion. Those who have been all through religious minded and have maintained this tendency even after mandatory retirement or attaining 60 years of age, do not face fast aging problems.

(iv) Further those senior citizens who emotionally feel the loss of social status and prestige or feel socially isolated and economically insecured after superannuation or 60 years of age, they experience fast aging problems.

(v) The higher the degree of personality and family disorganisation among the senior citizens, the deeper and sharper shall be the problems of aging.

(vi) The larger the extent of comprehensive social security and welfare measures to the elderly, the lesser shall be the intensity of aging problems to the senior citizens.

(vii) The larger the size of the family, more care the elderly receive.

(viii) The higher, the income of the elderly the higher is the status and power in the family and society.

Against hypothesis No. (i) the findings are:

(a) Cordial relations with the family members by 168(70%) respondents (Table 4.1).

(b) Further 194(81%) respondents do not at all feel socially alienated (Table 4.4).

(c) 175(73%) respondents report their participation in family functions regularly (Table 4.9).

On the basis of above findings we can safely accept the existence of a strong social bond as conceived by French Sociologist Emile Durkheim among the senior citizens under study. Naturally most of the respondents do not bother much about the aging problems.

As regards hypothesis No. (ii) in respect of continuity to work even alter 60 years of age or superannuation, we find two categories of respondents, i.e. elderly lawyers and doctors do not face many aging problems initially because of the continuity of their profession even after 60 years of age. The other two categories of superannuated university teachers and civil servants are the direct victims of the discontinuity to work/job/profession after 60 years of age and they face the economic problems and other consequential aging problems.

As regards hypothesis No. (iii) we find an increasing trend of regular worship of the deity/deities before and after superannuation or 60 years of age. Further there is a report of an increase in the number of worshippers among the superannuated university teachers and civil servants respectively from 48 per cent and 38 per cent before superannuation to 71 per cent and 70 per cent after superannuation (Table 6.15 Chapt. 6). This shows an increase of new worshippers after superannuation to the extent of 23 per cent and 32 per cent respectively among teachers and civil servants. As regards God's devotees among the elderly lawyers and doctors there is a fall in the percentage after 60 years of age front 77 per cent to 68 per cent among the elderly lawyers, i.e. by 9 per cent and from 93 per cent to 85 per cent among the elderly doctors, i.e. by 8 per cent (Table 6.15, Chapter 6). Although there is a tendency of decrease in the percentage of those performing religious activities among the elderly lawyers and doctors after 60 years of age but there are good number of elderly lawyers and doctors respectively as 68 per cent and 85 per cent (Table 6.17, Chapt. 6) still professing their faith in the Almighty and performing many religous rituals. On the whole we, therefore, find that most of the respondents under study are closely integrated with religious bond and this helps them in keeping carefree, fearless, depressionless, no worries and free from the pangs of fast aging.

As regards the hypothesis No. (iv) findings in support of the hypotheses Nos. (i), (ii) and (iii) conversely validate the present hypothesis that the respondents who are disintegrated and alienated from their social and religious bond and deprived of continuity to remunerative work after superannuation or 60 years of age, emotionally feel the loss of social and economic status and prestige, socially alienated and economically insecured.

In respect of hypothesis No. (v) the findings in support of hypotheses Nos. (i) and (iii) we feel a lesser degree of social, family and personality disorganisation among most of the respondents under study hence there is no question of acuter and sharper fast aging problems among the senior citizens.

So far hypothesis No. (vi) is concerned although the governmental agency has hardly provided adequate social security and welfare measures to the elderly for which there is a demand from the government on their part (in Tables Nos. 5.6 and 5.8, Chapter 5) but the respondents since young age have themselves made their own arrangement of social security measures and additional sources of income to such an extent that they do not feel much the pinch of economic distress and future security after superannuation or 60 years of age. Further most of the respondents 163(68%) anyhow have arranged their own houses because of their security minded feeling.

In response to the hypothesis No. (vii) there is a clear indication in Table 3.7, Chapter 3 that the majority of the respondents, i.e. 185(77%) live in Joint family naturally we can expect that most of the respondents are benefited with family care in old age.

The hypothesis No. (viii) is not validated in most of the cases of elderly respondents. There is considerable rise in the income groups of elderly doctors after 60 years of age hence due to economically well-off position they enjoy higher social status and power both in the family and society at large. On the other hand rest of the categories of respondents, i.e. superannuated university teachers, civil servants and elderly lawyers do not experience a rise in the income groups after superannuation or 60 years of age, hence having a lower economic status, are deprived of much of that social status and power in the family and society as that of elderly doctors.

Socio-Economic and Cultural Adjustments

The respondents age groups distribution is as 145(60%) in 60-70 years, 85(36%) in 71-80 years, and 10(4%) in 81years and above. Mostly 208(87%) respondents are Hindus by community. Their castewise distribution is 113 of higher castes, 84 of Middle castes and only 11 of lower castes category. After superannuation or 60 years of age the discontinuity to work affected specially superannuated 35(83%) teachers and 30(75%) civil servants by considerable reduction in their income groups. Among them only 7(17%) teachers and 10(25%) civil servants any how managed alternative remunerative job/works/ profession after superannuation. Due to discontinuity to work alter superannuation the reduction of income level has been reported upto Rs. 3 thousand p.m. by 25(60%) university teachers and upto the income level Rs. 5 to Rs.8 thousand p.m. by 25(62%) civil servants. Although there is continuity to work with the elderly lawyers but after attaining 60 years of age their total number against two lower income groups, i.e. upto Rs. 3 thousand p.m. and Rs. 3 to Rs. 5 thousand p.m. have risen respectively from 73(61%) to 80(67%) and from 17(14%) to 20(17%). Hence three categories of respondents, i.e. superannuated university teachers, civil servants, and the elderly lawyers have to bear upon the economic loss and related aging problems.

On the whole the respondents are mostly male (92%), married 84 per cent married. The majority of them 185(77%) live in joint family and 163(68%) own their houses. Further 70 per cent respondents report cordial relations with family members indicating a strong social tie helping them in making adjustment with many socio-economic and cultural problems.

As mostly younger members of the family generally remain away from the family due to their jobs and studies. These younger members make personal visit to the native home for couple of days in a year as reported by 44 per cent respondents hence very little chances of any family quarrel or tension during their brief stay on account of them with the elderly parents. In this short period they simply enquire from their elderly parents about their welfare. Consequently majority of respondents (81%) do not feel social alienation. It is only 19 per cent respondents feel social alienation because of contemptuous attitude of the family members (46%), due to conflicting values (17%) and minimum relations with others (17%).

Further there are 31% respondents who do not expect any physical and monetary help from their younger earning members hence they have no expectation of any sort of economic help or support from their own younger earning members. The majority of the respondents 54 per cent expect only emotional support from the younger and other family members. Further 73 per cent respondents report their regular participation in family functions. Inspite of so much conciliatory response toward the younger members of the family, these elderly respondents in good number 130(55%) report deprivation of social honour and power in the family. Such a humiliating situation is even reconciled with, without being irritated and "keeping mum" in all family bickering by 136(57%) elderly respondents.

Further the frequency of the respondents of the social calls with their friends and neighbours has now been considerably reduced after 60 years of age as reported by 68 per cent respondents. When asked about their liking for the continuity to work after 60 years of age, 229(95%) respondents report their preference for continuity to work either remunerative or non remunerative one. The reasons for this preference are for maintaining good health as reported by 163(68%), for financial need by 29(12%), a sort of engagement by 20(8%), for fulfilling left liabilities by 10(4%) and for enjoying social status and power by 7(3%).

Although 80(33%) respondents on the whole do not conceive of any evil consequence of discontinuity to work but the superannuated university teachers, civil servants and the elderly lawyers report evil effects of discontinuity to work after 60 years of age is fast physical aging by 62(26%), Depression by 38(16%), worries and tensions by 27(11%) and loss of socio-economic status by 8(4%).

In order to make the economic loss good the total number of 155(65%) respondents of all the three categories (university teachers, civil servants and the elderly lawyers) have managed additional sources of income after superannuation or 60 years of age. These additional sources are: Rent from shops, houses and vehicles as reported by 47(20%); hard earned savings by 43(18%), Income from alternative job/work/profession by 35(14%) and financial support from children by 30(13%). The economic problem becomes more acute if some of the liabilities remain unfulfilled after 60 years of age. These liabilities remaining unfulfilled are: Establishing their children/grandchildren in some job/work/profession as reported by 49(20%); Education of children/grandchildren/dependents by 28(12%), medical treatment by 29(8%); recurring expenses on cultivation work by 18(8%), building a new house or renovation of old house by 15(6%) and marriage of dependent children by 14(6%). In this respect there are fortunate respondents about 90(37%) reporting no liability left unfulfilled after 60 years of age.

As regards the adequacy of the present income after superannuation or 60 years of age we find disgusting reports from the respondents. A large number, i.e. 100(42%) consider their present income as 'Most Inadequate' respectively distributed among 29(69%) superannuated university teachers; 35(88%) superannuated civil servants, and 36(30%) elderly lawyers.

Considering the current income as only 'inadequate' by the total of 30(12%) respondents respectively distributed among 6(14%) superannuated university teachers, 5(12%) civil servants and 19(16%) elderly lawyers.

Considering the current income as 'Adequate' is reported by 53(44%) elderly lawyers, by few superannuated university teachers, i.e. 7(17%) and by 10(26%) by elderly doctors.

As regards considering the current income as "More than Adequate" it is mainly reported by 28(74%) elderly doctors and few well off, i.e. 12(10%) elderly lawyers.

The above findings clearly indicate that most of the elderly respondents feel economically depressed : hence they have many expectations from the government to help them in many walks of life. In this respect superannuated university teachers and civil servants chiefly insist on their demand for Higher pension, Income tax Relief, concession in Railway and Bus fares, free medical treatment, rebate and controlled price for food stuff and gas cylinder etc. and priority in house allotment. The elderly lawyers expect income tax relief, social insurance, income tax relief to those helping and supporting their elderly parents, free medical treatment, the elderly doctors expect chiefly income tax relief from the Government.

Bio-Psychological Problems and Adjustment

As regards physical aging problems most of the respondents suffer from some or the other physical trouble but largely 133(56%) respondents report eyesight trouble and the next one is Arthrite. Besides 62(26%) respondents do not experience the physical aging problems at all. On the whole 180(75%) report general physical debility. The main diseases they suffer from are (as reported) Cardiac problem by 21%, Arthrite by 12%, ENT trouble by 09%, Diabetis by 9% and Blood pressure by 7% etc.

Most of the respondents 125(52%) are vegetarian and take meals cooked generally by their spouses. Mostly respondents report normal duration of sleep i.e. from 6 to 8 flours.

Psychologically 64(27%) report depression and worries all the time due to contemptuous attitude of their family members. Similarly 145(60%) do not think about themselves as unwanted and worthless. They are generally very much optimistic and fully conscious about their utility and worth even after superannuation or 60 years of age.

In order to keep away the death phobia and enjoy complete physical and psychological security, various religious rituals and activities are performed by the respondents, in the hope of receiving God's blessings. These activities differ from person to person according to their convenience and faith as we find the habit of regular visit to a holy temple, church/mosque/Gurdwara etc. reported by 60 per cent narration of holy mantras and recitation of holy books daily by 60 per cent and attending religious discourses by 42 per cent among the superannuated teachers; Narration of holy mantras and recitation of religious books daily by 63 per cent, observing J*ap, Tap* and *Vrat* by 38 per cent, regularly visiting a holy place by 25 per cent, observing meditation and *yogasan* etc. among the superannuated civil servants; Narration of holy *mantras* and recitation of holy books daily by 67 per cent, regularly visiting a holy place by 42 per cent, and attending religious discourses by 42 per cent among the elderly lawyers; regularly visiting a holy place by 13 per cent, naration of *mantras* and recitation of holy books daily by 13 per cent and observing *Jap, Tap* and *Vrat* by 13 per cent among the elderly doctors.

In the various facets of mental and physical security in return of their above religious rituals and activities, they expect from God His blessings in the form of feeling like completely secured and protected by 70 per cent, Tie with community bond by 69 per cent, Full contentment by 63 per cent, Normal health by 59 per cent, Sweet and amiable relations with all by 58 per cent and No emotional problem by 50 per cent. This confirms the view that "the more religious minded the elderly are, the lesser shall be the feeling of intensity of aging problems". On the other hand we find that the majority of respondents, i.e. 208(87%) confirm the popular view that "one becomes more God fearing and religious in old age."

As regards respondents' leisure time activities as reported in order of preference are: Listening to Radio, cassetts and seeing television by 222 (93%), Morning/Evening walk by 170(71%), Recitation of holy books by 155(65%), Reading Newspapers, Novels, Magazines, New Publications and current professional journals by 150(63%) and writing letters, Articles, Reports, Preparing Notes and writing poems etc. by 110(46%).

Quite contrary to the popular sentiments of settling down in the native home and place after superannuation or 60 years of age we find 177(74%) respondents do not prefer settling down at their native village home for various reasons. On the other hand we find 160(67%)

prefer living with their sons and very few 29(12%) prefer to live in Old Age Home. There is a strong dislike for living in Old Age Home. In this respect 198(83%) respondents are against living in Old Age Homes. There are only 42 such respondents wishing to join some Old Age Home only because of three reasons viz., Contemptuous attitude of the family members, Not to have any obligation for care and support from family members, the destitute respondents finding none to lookafter them after superannuation or sixty years of age.

As regards main problems of aging, 180(75%) respondents report Physical debility, Family tension by 145(60%), Loneliness by 115(48%), Economic problem by 110(46%), Worries and tensions by 105(44%), Death phobia by 95(40%) and Dependency by 87(36%).

When asked from the respondents about their chief demands from the government about their welfare and security we find in order of preference: Separate counters at the public places for them by 237%(99%), Subsidy in essential consumption goods and articles of daily use by 210(88%), Concession and Rebates etc. in prices of commodities of daily use by 205(85%), Mobile medical help at their residence by 202(84%), Separate Geriatric ward in District Civil Hospital, Medical College and Health centres by 202(84%), Remunerative engagement utilising their expertise, skill and excellence by 175(13%). Membership in Government, Committees, Commissions for the welfare of the elderly by 145(60%) and Timebound revision of pension by 82(34%).

Suggestions

In order to reduce the aging problems of the senior citizens such as biological, i.e. health problems, arising out of their advancing age, the economic problem due to the reduction in the income level and psychosocial and cultural problems arising due to their participation in social cultural activities and life in the modern family, the following ways and means of their mitigation seem to be more wise, useful and highly redeeming:

(a) Geriatric wards are to be opened in every District hospital. Orientation courses should be arranged for the doctors in the field of Geriatric medicine.

(b) If possible, domiciliary services, should be provided for the sick and infirm.

(c) The elderly (60+) who require regular treatment like taking Insulin, checking BP etc., para-medical staff be provided for their care.

(d) The family members should be made aware of the psychological and health problems of the elderly in such a way that they should take a sympathetic attitude towards the old.

(e) Facilities be provided to rehabilitate the incapacitated elderly who are a burden to the family and those who are left alone when the family members go out for work or for other purposes.

(f) The Government should give incentive to families which take care of the elderly like Income tax relief and posting those in places of their residence where they can lookafter their elderly parents well.

(g) The elderly (60+) physically and mentally fit to work should be helped in finding out some remunerative work, full time or part time, in the field of their interest and ability. This will help them in reducing their feeling of dependency on others as well as unwantedness.

(h) As the trend in the developing world like India however is in a somewhat different direction, the cultural norm of taking care of the elderly parents is undergoing erosion. Hence the family should be strengthened as the primary Care giver to ensure comprehensive welfare of senior citizens. In this task state, community and the NGOs should be required to play more active role.

(i) Concept of health promotion and preventive geriatrics should be popularized among the masses for effective healthy aging of the population at large.

(j) In view of the increased life expectancy and its projected further increase in the coming years and the fitness of the elderly at sixty and onward, knowledge and experience of elderly should be more actively utilized. Elderly should be involved in income generating schemes. They should be organized and empowered to increase their bargaining power. Various subsidies, concessións and facilities be provided to them

(k) Community homes for the elderly destitute should be established and subsidized food and other essentials should be extended to the elderly who belong to weaker sections of the population. Old age pension be raised reasonably.

(l) Special attention be given to the elderly women and the widows.

(m) The government should further seriously consider free or at least subsidized facilities for the elderly in travel to their relatives, friends and religious places.

(n) The preference for housing allotment to those who bring their old parents in urban areas. If any family maintains an elderly who is bed-ridden, the bread winner of the family should be completely exempted from Income tax.

(o) Minister of Social Welfare, New Delhi should make provision for an Identity Card for all elderly persons for receiving benefits of various social security schemes of the Government.

(p) A National Institute of Ageing should be established and studies on the elderly should be declared a priority area of research. A National policy for the welfare of the elderly should be formulated.

In the Planning Commission the Centre should constitute a National Committee on Aging to discuss analyse and recommend certain Policy issues in the Parliament. The inputs of this committee should come from the proposed Apex Institute, viz. National Institute of Aging. The terms of reference of this National Level Institute should be:

(a) to identify and focus on the aged as a vulnerable group,

(b) to encourage greater participation of non-governmental organization in the care of the aged, particularly through running Day Care Centres,

(c) to promote various schemes of social security for the elderly specially in the unorganised sector, and

(d) to consider the elderly as an asset to promote to the utilization of their potential for community development in organising themselves.

National Policy for the Elderly in India

In view of the demands and expectations of the respondents under-study there is an inevitable need for a suitable National policy for the elderly in India. The United Nations General Assembly adopted principles for elderly persons on 16th December, 1991 to encourage governments to design their own policies and programmes in this regard. The guiding principles of this resolution were: Independence, Participation, Care and Self Fulfilment.

In August 1998, The National Policy for older persons was formulated by the Central Government tracing recent trends, it recognised demographic aging as a global phenomenon that has hit Indian shores. The macro and household implications of this phenomenon both economic and social, were considered. The policy seeks to assure older persons that their concerns are national concerns and that they will not continue to live unprotected, ignored or marginalised. Under the policy the state is to:

(i) extend support for financial security (pensions, provident funds, taxation policies, long-term saving instruments, employment after superannuation, simplification of maintenance laws etc.), health care and nutrition (affordability, subsidisation, public health care, health insurance, promoting developments, hospitals and other facilities like health, education etc.), shelter (urban and rural lousing schemes, civic amenities etc.), education (training and information, non-discrimination, aging information, etc.), welfare (promotion of voluntary organisation involved in helping the elderly), setting up of welfare funds etc.,
(ii) provide protection against their abuse and exploitation,
(iii) make available opportunities for development of the potential of the elderly, and
(iv) seek their participation and offer for their services so that they can improve the quality of their lives.

The above proposed National Policy for the senior citizens in India is based on certain principles which are:

(i) Recognition of the need for affirmative action in favour of the elderly,
(ii) Recognition of the value of an Age-integrated society where bonds between the young and the old are strong.
(iii) Recognition that elderly persons, too, are a Resource.
(iv) Belief to the empowerment of older persons enabling them

to acquire better control over their lives and participate in decision-making on matters which affect them as well as on other issues as equal partners in the development process.

(v) Recognition that larger budgetary allocation from the State is necessary.

(vi) Emphasis on the need for expansion of social and community services for older persons.

(vii) Recognition of the role of media in identifying emerging issues and areas of action in aging problems among the elderly in India.

(viii) Emphasis on implementation (the Ministry of Social Justice and Development) will coordinate a National Council for older persons. Panchayati Raj Institutions be encouraged to participate in implementation of welfare schemes for the elderly. Annual and Five Year Action plans are to be prepared by each Ministry to implement aspects which concern them.

Policy Suggestions

(i) Research be conducted to elucidate the etiology, pathogenesis and therapy of disorders common among the elderly.

(ii) Efforts be made to develop standard elderly population survey instruments which may be included in the Census Survey.

(iii) With increase in longevity, the post-retirement period is going to equal or exceed the period of active service. Two factors need to be considered in this regard:

(a) enhancement of retirement age universally applicable to the Central and State Government employees, and

(b) effective utilization of elders.

Here new job opportunities for the elderly need to be located by analysing the existing labour markets. Elderly persons should have a right to productive employment. Policy should therefore facilitate the building of the capacity of local communities to allow participation of elderly persons in community driven, economic development initiatives.

(iv) Where feasible, community based supportive services for the elderly should be developed in partnership with family members, with the help of local institutions such as Panchayati Raj, local resources and the skills of the elderly persons themselves.

(v) While formulating policies for the elderly, experiences and examples can be drawn from the social security policies of other countries like Japan, Canada and China.

(vi) In the present changing social scenario we are vested with onerous task of strengthening the institution of family by bringing about modifications in it because the family by far still remains the best as far as providing appropriately compassionate and human care to the senior citizens.

(vii) Another area which holds promise is of reviving the time tested concept of the Ashrams which should be suitably adapted and modified.

(viii) Certain categories of elderly persons particularly doctors and lawyers can be considered for re-employment under different governmental departmental programmes like Adult Education, Health Education, Family Planning, Local Self Government (Nyaya Panchayat) relief work etc. on a part-time basis since they are respectable persons and acceptable to a majority of the people. This will enhance, the process of their adjustment and make them feel as valued members of the society.

(ix) Further it would be necessary to educate the elderly people to take the necessary preventive and curative measures so that they can lead a healthy life in later years. Implementation of the 'Health Insurance Scheme' by LIC is a welcome step in this regard.

(x) The present system of health care is mostly confined to the clinic or the hospital. For receiving such services old people depend on their children. It is difficult for old people to climb steps, to walk long distances, to travel in over-crowded buses to reach urban health care centres. Hence Health care for the elder is arranged periodically in their own houses.

(xi) In view of the various post-retirement problems it is desirable to make arrangements for free counselling to the old about how to regulate life in their situations.

(xii) State, Community and the NGOs should be required to play more active role in this effort.

(xiii) Community homes for the destitute elderly should be established.

(xiv) Lastly, a National Institute of Aging be established and studies on the elderly be declared a priority area of research.

Appendix

INTERVIEW SCHEDULE

UGC Sponsored Major Research Project on "Aging Among the Senior Citizens"—A Sociological study of the problems of aging among the superannuated civil servants, University Teachers, Lawyers and Doctors.

This is a sociological study of Aging among four categories of the senior citizens, viz. superannuated civil servants, and university teachers; and lawyers and doctors of 60+ of Gorakhpur district in Eastern Uttar Pradesh.

In the pages that follow you will find a list of questions dealing with various aspects of the problem of aging generally common to all the above mentioned four categories of senior citizens. You are requested to answer all questions you consider relevant to you. Your free and frank answer will be highly appreciated. The replies would remain anonymous and will be kept confidential.

You do not need to be told that the findings of this project would be of considerable use for social scientists and the Government in framing a suitable policy for the welfare of the elderly, in the state and the country.

Your kind cooperation is, therefore, solicited.

INTERVIEW SCHEDULE

(A) Identification Data

1. (a) Name ____________________ (b) Sex M/F ________________
   (c) Age ____________ Years (d) Caste ____________________
   (e) Religion ______________ (f) Education __________________
   (g) Address (Local) ____
   (Permanent) ____
2. What was your profession/Occupation before superannuating or attaining 60 years of age ________________
3. Present profession/occupation, if any (after superannuation or attaining 60 years of age) ________________
4. Income

Income Group [in 000(thousand) Rs. p.m.]	*Before Superannuation/attaining 60 years of age*	*After Superannuation/ attaining 60 years of age*
Upto Rs. 3 thousand p.m.		
Rs. 3 to Rs. 5 thousand p.m.		
Rs.6 to Rs. 15 thousand p.m.		
Rs.16 to Rs. 25 thousand p.m.		
Rs. 26 to Rs. 35 thousand p.m.		
Rs. 36 to Rs. 45 thousand p.m.		
Rs. 46 to Rs. 55 thousand p.m.		
Rs. 56 thousand and above. p.m.		

5. Sources of Income

	Before Superannuation/Attaininy 60 yrs of age	*After Superannuation/Attaining 60 years of age*
Salary		
Consultation Fee		
Pension		
Honorarium		
Interest from Savings		
Commission		
Tuition		
Coaching		
Guiding Fee		
New/Additional/Alternative Job		
Remuneration		
Rent From Landed Property		

Income from sale of Agricultural Products
Earning from running :
- (a) Taxi services
- (b) Auto
- (c) Jeep
- (d) Truck
- (e) Tractor
- (f) Tullu Pump

Royalty on Books and Guide books
Earning From New/Additional :
- (a) Clinics
- (b) Centres
- (c) Establishment

---

6. Current Marital Status : Never Married/Married/Widow/Widower/Separated
7. If currently married, does your spouse (husband/wife) live with you in this house now ? ----- Yes ----No
8. Family --------- Joint ------- Extended -------- Nuclear.
9. How many children do you have ? (from all your marriages)

	Male	Female
	________	________
(a) Total Number born		
(b) Total number alive	________	________
(c) Number living in your house	________	________
(d) Number living elsewhere	________	________

10. How many were your brothers and sisters ?
    - (a) Born Brother ------ Sister ------
    - (b) Alive ------- ------
11. Do you live in a house of your:
    -------- own/ -------- rented/ --------Neighbour's/--------
12. If you were in legal/medical profession, at which age would you consider as the proper time for retiring from active professional work.

At the age of	Commence retiring	Completely retired
50 yrs	--------	-------
58 yrs	--------	-------
60 yrs	--------	-------
65 yrs	--------	-------
70 yrs	--------	-------
75 yrs and above	--------	-------
Never.	--------	-------

13. What will be your considerations for retiring from the profession? Senility -------------/Failing health -------------/Availability of a successor to continue your family profession ------------/ any other reason (specify) -----------/
14. At what age you think one should normally start reducing working hours. -------Years of age.
15. Have you taken, complete retirement from your profession ?
    Yes---------------/No--------------- If yes---------------

(i) because you now want to spend your old age in peace and devote the rest of life to religious pursuits
(ii) because you suffer from some kind of physical debility
(iii) any other reason.

16. Do you wish now to engage yourself in any other activity such as social service etc. Yes-------/No-----
If yes, please specify the intended sphere of activity-------------

(B) Social and Cultural Adjustments

17. With whom do you live in your family?
With------------ husband/wife/------------ own sons and daughters/------------ /--------------/Grandsons and daughters/brothers and sisters/-------------- Nephews and Nieces/--------------- brothers wife/wives sons and daughters/-- ------------with in-laws.
18. How are your relations with your family members?
-------------- cordial/ ---------------normal/ ---------------uncordial/------------- strained.
19. Your sons and daughters not live with you in the home?
If yes, it is because of : ---------------Yes/---------------No
(a) Their step-mother in the house --------------
(b) Being employed at distant places ---------------
(c) Shortage of accommodation in the house --------------
(d) Your drinking habit --------------
20. If your children, not staying with you, do the following :

	Rarely	Often	Never
(a) Visit you	--------	--------	--------
(b) Write letters to you	--------	--------	--------
(c) Send presents	--------	--------	--------

21. If your brothers/sisters who are away and do not stay with you, do the following

	Rarely	Often	Never
(a) Visit you	--------	--------	--------
(b) Write letters to you	--------	--------	--------

22. Do you feel alienated due to the least interaction with the family members and others in the community?
-----------Always/-----------most of the time/-----------sometimes/---------never
23. If always, it is because of :
(a) Indifferent attitude of family members ----------
(b) Conflict of values with those of younger generations ----------
(c) Adverse relations with the children/grandchildren ----------
(d) Minimum relations with the neighbours and friends ----------
24. What is the frequency of contact in between you and your family members?
----------Regular/----------Often/----------Occasional/----------No contact
25. Which type of support and help do you expect from your children/grand-children after superannuation or post 60 years of age?
----------Physical/----------Monetary/----------Social/----------Emotional-------- --not at all expecting any support/

26. Who amongst the following takes care of you after superannuation or post-60 years of age?
    (a) You had only sons and they do or do not take care of you ----------Yes/----------No
    (b) You had only daughters and they do or do not take care of you ----------Yes/----------No
    (c) Both sons and daughters take care of you ----------Yes/----------No
    (d) You need no care from anybody ----------Yes/----------No
27. With whom would you like to converse with most?
    With-----------wife/husband/ ----------children/ ----------Grandchildren/----------relatives/ ----------neighbours/----------friends.
28. Do you participate in family functions?
    ----------Always/ ----------Most of the time/ ----------Sometimes/ ----------Never
29. If never, it is because of :
    (a) Fear of bickering among the family members ----------
    (b) Family members dislike your participation ----------
    (c) Considering performing family function an expensive affair ----------
    (d) On health ground ----------
30. Do your family member honour your words and obey your commands?
    ---------- Always/ ----------Most of the time/----------Sometimes/----------Never
31. Do you feel irritated with the reactions and responses of your family members?
    ----------Always/----------most of the time irritated/ ----------only sometimes -------/never feel irritated.
32. How do you adjust or reconcile with undesirable reactions of your family members?
    ----------By yielding/----------keeping mum/----------Not meddling with family affairs------becoming submissive even to the youngsters------remaining outside the house for some time.
33. Did you have any close friends/colleagues?
    ----------Yes/----------No
34. If yes, how often did you meet them before and after superannuation or 60 years of age?

	Frequently	More frequently	Less frequently	Never
Before Superannuation or 60 years of age	-------	--------	--------	--------
After superannuation or post-60 years of age	-------	--------	--------	--------

35. Do any of your former collegue/friend see you at home?
    If yes, how often-----------frequently/-----------more frequently/----------- less frequently/-----------never.
36. What do you converse most about when you meet your old friend/colleague?
    ------family matters/------social affairs/------ economic problems/------public issues/------social security measures.

(C) Economic Adjustments

37. Do you like, if possible to continue the work even after superannuation or attaining 60 years of age ?
    ------Yes/------No

38. If yes, it is because of : ------normal health/------financial need/-----a sort of engagement/------in view of retaining social status and power.
39. What was the impact of any of sudden loss of income, power and professional status after superannuation—
------Started aging fast/------losing normal stamina and zest for life/------Always worrying/------always in search of an alternative remunerative/ non-remunerative job/activity.
40. If you are a pensioner, is the amount of pension adequate enough to meet your basic needs ?
------Yes/------No
41. Can you adequately support your wife/husband, dependent children and other dependents, if any, on your present monthly income ?
------Yes/------No
42. If not then how do you manage to meet their expenses?
------doing any remunerative job/------from hard earned savings/ ------from other sources.
43. Do you have financial liabilities at present and/or likely to have in the near future ?
------Yes/------No

If yes, then specify:
------education of children/------marriage of sons/daughters and other dependents/------building a house or renovation of old house /------purchasing some land/------meeting medical expenses.
44. Do you have some sources to fall back upon in times of meeting contingencies.
------Yes/------No

If yes, then specify the sources:
------P.F. and Gratuity/ ------NSC/------Indira Vikas Patra/---Kisaan Vikas Patra/ -----LIC/------Postal LIC/------Recurring Deposits in Bank/P.O./------FDR in Bank/ ------UTI Shares/---Gold a Silver Ornaments/------Landed property/----- Rented house/shops------Interest and Dividends on Shares.
45. Whom do you look for financial support in times of need ?
------Children/------Grandchildren/------Relatives/-----friends/------ neighbours/ ------Government agency/------Non-Government Agency/------none.
46. What are your economic expectations from the Government ?
------higher pension/------financial exemptions/------concession in rail and bus fares/------priority in medical facilities/------free passes for places of recreation/ ------priority in railway reservation/------fuel gas/ ------ration of food/ ------priority in the allotment of house to the senior citizens/ -----concession to the dependents of the senior citizens/ ------tax rel ef on monetary award to those helping /serving the senior citizens.

(D) Bio-Psychological Adjustments

47. Do you have any of the following problems ?
(a) See properly Yes/No
(b) Hear properly Yes/No
(c) Walk properly Yes/No

48. If yes, then Financed/Managed by whom

	Self	Children/ Grand-children brother/ sister	Other Relativ-es	Govern-ment Age-ncy	Volunt-ary Ag-ency
(a) Glasses - Yes/No	---	---	---	---	---
(b) Hearing Aid -Yes/No	---	---	---	---	---
(c) Walking Stick-Yes/No	---	---	---	---	---
(d) Dentures - Yes/No	---	---	---	---	---
(e) Wheel chair - Yes/No	---	---	---	---	---
(f) Footwear - Yes/No	---	---	---	---	---

49. How is your health ?
------on the whole good/------Occasional minor illness/ ------ Occasional general disability/------Chronic disease/ ------ sudden serious illness.
50. Diseases you suffer from at this age of your life—
------None/------some trouble in ENT/ ------Arthritis/-----Asthama/-----Blood pressure/------heart trouble/------ skin/ ------diabetic/------General weakness/ ------hard of hearing/ ------seeing/------physically handicapped/----- psychiatric problem/------Prostrate gland/------Rheumatic trouble/ ----any other.
51. Which type of treatment do you prefer ?
------Allopathic/------Homeopathic/------Ayurvedic/------ Any other (specify).
52. Do you require help or support for the following :

	No need of any help	*Need help*	*Cannot do even with help*
(a) Getting out of bed	---	---	---
(b) Bathing	---	---	---
(c) Walking inside the house	---	---	---
(d) Walking for some distance	---	---	---
(e) Taking food	---	---	---
(f) Dressing	---	---	---
(g) Going to the toilet	---	---	---

53. Do you have any perennial health problem ?
-------Yes/-------No.
54. If you fall sick will you consult a doctor ?
-------Yes/-------No.

If no, what are the reasons ?
(a) ------ you have no money
(b) ------No body to bring a doctor or take you to the doctor
(c) ------ Doctor cannot help you
(d) ------Doctor is far away
If yes, who paid for the medicine and medical consultation ?
(a) ------self/ (b) ------ children (c) ------other relatives/
(d) ------Neighbours (e) ------ reimbursed.

55. How many hours do you sleep every day ? ------ hrs.
56. How is your appetite ?
    ------ very good / ------ good / ------ fair /------ bad.
57. Do you prepare your own food or does someone else help you in preparing the food ?
    (a) ------ prepare yourself/ (b) ------ prepared by wife/husband/ (c) ------ children/ (d) ------ cook / (e) ------ relatives/ (d) ------ others.
58. When and with whom you take meals in the house
    (a) ------ Alone first/------ Alone last/------ with children / ------ with Grand-children.
59. Are you vegetarian / Non-vegetarian ?
    Vegetarian ------Yes/------No.
    Non-vegetarian ------ Yes/------No.
60. Do you feel yourself unwanted and a useless creature due to old age and also feel that life is not worth living now ?
    ------Yes/------No.

    If yes, it is due to :
    (a) discontinuity of work -------
    (b) Neglect and open disrespect from youngsters -----
    (c) Want of economic support from your family -----
    (d) Loss of status, power and social recognition ------
61. Do you believe in God ? ------Yes/------No.
    If yes, how have you been living to that belief ?
    (a) Have been worshipping God since long -------
    (b) Visiting temple of your deity regularly ------
    (c) Attending religious discourses of great saints from time to time ------
    (d) Organising religious functions at own residence from time to time -------
62. Do you think your religious faith has served the needs of your life well ?
    ------Yes/------No.

    If yes, in what tangible form :
    (a) You have no worry -------
    (b) No deprivation -------
    (c) enjoy social prestige -----
    (d) full peace and contentment ------
    (e) No emotional problem at all -----
    (f) Feel fully secured and protected -------
    (g) enjoy normal health --------
    (h) have smooth and sweet relations with all -----
63. How do you spend your leisure time ?
    (a) Doing nothing nor capable of doing anything ------
    (b) Doing nothing though capable of doing a lot -----
    (c) Reading novels/magazines/New publications of interest/ newspapers ------
    (d) Listening to radio/deck -------
    (e) Seeing the television --------
    (f) Writing letters/articles/academic reports ---------.
    (g) Practising *yoga/japa* (repetition of Gods' name) all the time -----
    (h) Participation in religious gatherings -------
    (i) Indoor games -------

(j) Rendering social service ------
(k) Morning, Evening walk/visiting daily/weekly(monthly a holy place -----
(1) singing/gardening/painting/gossiping --------

64. It is said that children are the main support for the parents in old age. Do you agree with this view ?
------Yes/------No.
65. Do you think that the youngsters of the present generation have less respect for the elderly ?
------Yes/------No.
66. Some retired persons feel that one is more dependent on one's husband/wife/ sons/daughter etc. in one's old age, what is your view about it ?
67. ------Agree/------disagree/------Indecisive/------No opinion
68. Do you feel that one becomes more and more religious in old age ?
------Yes/------No.
69. Do you have any landed property at your native place ?
------Yes/------No.
70. Are you now planning to settle down at your native place after superannuation or attaining 60 years of age ?
------Yes/------No.
If no then, why not ? (a)-------------/(b)--------------/(c)---------------
71. Are you aware of the existence of Old Age Homes ?
------ Yes/ -----No
72. Which in your opinion is the best place for persons to live in their old age ?
------with sons/----------with daughters/------Alone/-----in an Old Age Home/ Day Care Centre.
73. Are you willing to join an Old Age Home ? ------Yes/------No
If yes, it is so because of the cold and contemptuous attitude of your sons and daughter-in-law in the house?
------ Yes/ -----No.
If yes, will you be able to bear the cost of being an inmate of an Old Age Home ?
If no, then how do you plan to meet your expenses in the Old Age Home ?
74. Do you think that your family members will appreciate your living in an old Age Home ?
------Yes/------No.
75. What are the unpleasant aspects of your personal life ?
(a) Disrespect from family members ---------
(b) Separation from children/grand children --------
(c) Loneliness ---------
(d) Socially alienated --------
(e) Bad Health ---------
(f) Dependency ----------
(g) Feeling yourself unwanted ----------
(h) None cares, helps and utters some consolatory words ---------
(i) None to pay attention to your personal feelings and desires ----------
76. Do you feel depressed ? ------Yes/------No
If yes, it is because of :
(a) Declining social-cultural values ---------

(b) Frequent shift of residence -------
(c) Restrictions on mobility --------
(d) Bereavement -------
(e) Inadequate social contact --------

77. What are your main desires and wishes ?
(a) Peaceful and contented life ------
(b) Recognition and expect sweet response from all -------
(c) Be in the company of devotees of God -------
(d) Normal health --------
(e) No dependency -------
(f) Own work by self -------
(g) Economically well-off ------
(h) Fulfil all the liabilities of life ------
(i) Sweet home with sweet people -------
(j) Natural death ---------

79. In your opinion which are the main problems of aging ?
(a) ----- Physical problem (b) ------- Family tensions (c) --------death phobia (d) ------ feeling loneliness / (e) ------- all the time perturbed / (f) ------ fear of untoward event all the time / (g) ------ economic problem/ (h) ------ feeling socially alienated.

80. In what way do you think the government can help the elderly ?
(a) Increasing the rate and amount of present pension p.m.-----
(b) Granting concessions and exemptions of different sorts to the senior citizens -------
(c) Reserved quota for Senior Citizens in the Committees and Commissions relating to the welfare of the elderly -----
(d) Extending subsidies in essential necessities of life to the senior citizens ------
(e) Establishing Separate Counters for the Senior Citizens in Public Places ------
(f) Separate reserved places in Bus/Railway/Hospital -------------
(g) Remunerative jobs of skill and excellence --------
(h) Granting subsidies for installing a new plant/centre/Institution etc. in the private sector -------
(i) Government financed and managed Old Age Home/day care centres etc.--------

BIBLIOGRAPHY

Adler, W.H., 1974 : A autoimmune theory of aging, In M. Rockstein, M.L. Sussman and J. Chesky, eds., *Theoretical Aspects of Aging,* Academic Press, New York.

Aiken, Lewis, R., 1995 : *Aging – An Introduction to Gerontology.*

Atchley, Robert, C. 1976 : *The Sociology of Retirement.* Scheukman Publishing Co., New York.

Agnihotri, Harendra Kumar, 1976 : 'Problems of the Old Age'. *Agra University Journal of Research,* 24(2), July 1976.

Ainlay, S.C. and Smith, D.R., 1984 : Aging and religious participation, *Journal of Gerontology,* 39(3), pp. 357-363.

Anantharaman, R.N., 1982 : The problems of the older people in a changing society, *Journal of the Madras University,* LIV.2, pp.31-33.

——1983 : Age-old respect for the aged in India, *Yojana,* 27(1-2) pp. 57-60.

Baltes, P.B. and Schaie, K.W. 1974 : The myth of the twilight years, *Psychology Today,* 7(10), pp. 35-40.

Baum, S.K., 1982 : Loneliness in elderly persons : A preliminary study, *Psychological Reports,* 50(3), pp. 1313-1318.

Bengston, V.L. 1973 : *The social psychology of aging,* Bobbs Merrill, New York.

Bhatia, H.S., 1983 : *Aging and Society : A sociological study of the retired public servants.* Arya Book Centre, Udaipur.

Birren, J.E., 1964 : *The Psychology of Aging*, Prentice Hall, Englewood Cliffs, N.J.

Birren, J.E. and Remer, V.J. 1977 : 'Research on the psychology of Aging : Principles and Experimentation'. In J.E. Birren and L.W. Schaie, eds., *Handbook of the Psychology of Aging,* Van Nostrand Reinhold, New York.

Bose, A.B. and Gangrade, K.D., 1989 : *Aging in India : Problems and Potentials,* Abhinav Publications, New Delhi.

Bhatia, H.S., 1983 : *Aging and Society,* Arya Book Centre, Udaipur.

Bhatt, R.N., 1983 : *Indian Express,* February, 18.

Birren, J.E. 1959 : *Handbook of Aging and the Individual.* Chicago University Press.

Biswas, H.S., 1987 : *Aging in Contemporary India,* Indian Anthropological Society, Calcutta.

Bytheway, Bill., Keil, Teresa, Allatt, Patriciae a Bryman, Alein, (eds.), 1990 : *Becoming and Being old Sociological Approaches to Laterlife,* Sage Publications, London.

Chanana, H.B. and P.P. Talwar, 1987 : 'Aging in India : Its Socio-economic and Health Implications', *Asia Pacific Population Journal,* Vol. 2, No.3, pp. 23-38.

Chandra Dave, 1983 : 'Some Psycho-social Aspects of Aging'. Paper presented at the National Seminar on Psychosocial Aspects of Aging, Tirupati.

Chandra, Sekhariah, 1985 : 'Problems of issues in Aging'. Papers on International Seminar on Population Aging in India. University Department of Sociology, University of Kerala, Trivandrum.

Dhaon, J.K., *et al.* 1983 : Some bio-social characteristics of pensioners of Lucknow city, *Health and Population,* 6(2), pp. 119-27.

Desai, K.N. and R.D. Naik, 1971 : 'Problems of Retired People in Greater Bombay'. Tata Institute of Social Sciences, No-27, Bombay.

D'Souza, Alfred, 1982 : *Aging in South Asia,* India Social Institute Monograph Series, New Delhi.

D'Souza, V.S., 1974 : 'Changes in Social Structure and Changing Roles of Older People in India', *Sociology and Social Research,* Vol. 55 Nos., April.

Desai, K.G. and Rekha Bhalla, 1978 : *Social Situation of the Aged.* Tata Institute of Social Sciences, Bombay.

D'Souza, V.S. 1989 . 'Changing Social Scene and Its Implication for the Aged', in K.G. Desai (ed.) *Aging in India,* Ashish Publishing House, New Delhi.

Dhillon, P.K., 1992 : *Psycho-social Aspects of Aging in India,* Concept Publishing Company, New Delhi.

Dandekar, Kumudini, 1996 : *The Elderly in India,* Sage Publications, New Delhi.

Goyal, R.S., 1989 : 'The Problem of Aging', *Population Education News,* Vol. 15, No.6, pp. 4-8.

Gulati, Leela and S. Irudaya Rajan, 1991 : 'Social and Economic Implications of Population Aging in Kerala, India', *Social Development Issues,* Vol.13, No.3, Spring. pp.90-99.

Gangrade, K.D., 1989 : 'Emerging Conception of Aging in India: Socio-Cultural Perspective'. Lucknow . *The Eastern Anthropologist,* Vol. 42, No.2.

Golpelwar, V.M. 1964 : 'Problems of the Aged in Changing Patterns of Society'. Tata Institute of Social Sciences, Bombay.

Ghosal, B.C., 1982 : Care of the Aged, *Yojana*, 26(10), pp.9-10.

Ghosal, L.K., 1982 : Facts about old persons, *Yojana,* 26(10) pp.7-8.

Gomatinayagam, V.,1987 : The problems of the aged in Urban India - A study in the Union Territory of Pondicherry, *Indian Journal of Community Guidance Service,* 4(1), pp.71-88.

Hobman David, 1971 : *The Social challenge of Aging.* Croom Helm Ltd., London.

Irudaya Rajan, S. and U.S. Mishra, 1995 : 'Defining old Age: An Indian Assessment', *Journal of United Nations Institute on Aging,* Malta, Vol.5, No. 4, pp. 31-35.

Irudaya Rajan, S. and U.S. Mishra, 1997 : 'Population Aging : Causes and Consequences', in K.C. Zachariah and S.Irudaya Rajan (eds) *Kerala's Demographic Transition: Determinants and Consequences,* Sage Publications, New Delhi, pp. 222-36.

Irudaya Rajan, S., U.S. Mishra and P.S. Sharma, 1995 : 'An Agenda for National Policies on Aging in India'. *Research and Development Journal,* (Journal of Help Age India), Vol. 1, No. 2, pp. 38-53.

Johnson, Elizabeth S. and John B. Williamson, 1980 : *The Social Problems of Aging,* Holt., Rinehart and Winston, New York.

John, Palen, 1979 : *Social Problems of Aging.* McGraw-Hill Book Company, New York.

Kumar, Sanjay, 1991 : 'Aging of Population: An Investigation in Indian Context', in Indira Jai Prakash (ed.) *Quality Aging,* Association of Gerontology (India), Varanasi, pp. 55-75.

Kumar, S. Vijaya, 1991 : *Family Life and Socio-Economic Problems of Aged.* Ashish Publishing House, Delhi.

Kullai Reddy, L., 1984 : 'A Study of the Attitudes towards Aging and Their Relation to the Problems of Adjustment of Older People'. (Unpublished). M. Phil Dissertation, S.V. University, Tirupati.

Kelkar, Vasundhara, 1974 : 'A psychological study of the problem of old age adjustment', M.A. Dissertation, S.P. College, Pune.

Kumar, Vinod, 1996 : 'Aging Indian Perspective and Global Scenario', Published by Prof. Vinod Kumar, Department of Medicine, AIMS, New Delhi.

Kullai, Reddy, L. and Ramamurti, P.V., 1988 : 'Attitude towards aging, *Journal of Psychological Researches,* 32 (1-2), pp. 82-84.

Kasthoori, R. (Dr.), 1996 : *The Problems of the Aged—A Sociological Study,* Uppal Publishing House, New Delhi.

Mahadevan, K., 1986 : 'A System of Policy for Welfare of the Elderly Citizens'. *Indian Journal of Social Work,* Vol. XLVI, No.4, Bombay.

Mathew Philip, M., 1990 : 'Taking Care of the Aged'. *The Hindu* (dt. 16.1.90).

Mishra, Saraswati, 1988 : *Social adjustment in old age,* B.R. Publications, Delhi.

Moberg, D.O., 1970 : 'Religiosity in old Age', *The Gerontologist* 5(2), pp. 78-87.

Ministry of Social Welfare, Government of India, 1982 : *The Aged in India,* World Assemby on Aging, Vienna, 26th July - 6th August.

National Sample Survey Organisation, 1991 : 'Socio-Economic Profile of the Aged Persons : NSS 42nd Round (July 1986 - June 1987)', *Servekshana,* Vol. 15, No.2, New Delhi.

Moody Harry, R., 1998 : *Aging Concepts and Controversies,* Fine Forge Press, A Sage Publications Company, Thousand Oaks.

Nayar, P.K.B., 1985 : 'Population Aging in India : The Background'. Paper Presented at the International Seminar on Population Aging in India, Trivandrum.

Nirmala, S. 'A Study of the Aged and Attitudes of Adolescent Towards the Aged in Tirupati', Unpublished Ph.D. Dissertation, S.V. University of Tirupati, 1969.

Natrajan, V.S. 1987 : Geriatrics : A new discipline in India, *Indian Journal of Community Guidance Service,* 4(1), pp. 63-70.

Pathak, J.D., 1980 : *Our Elderly.* Tata Institute of Social Sciences, Bombay.

Pathi, R.N. and Jena, B. (Ed.), 1989 : *Aged in India.* Ashish Publishing House, New Delhi.

Pillai, A.K.B., 1986 : 'The Asian Indian Model of the Elderly: A Study in Indian Anthropological Gerontology'. *Journal of the Indian Anthropological Society,* Vol.20, No.3, Calcutta.

Pollack, O., 1949 : 'Social Adjustment in old Age.' *Social Science Research Council Bulletin,* No.59.

Peplau, L. and Perlman, D., 1982, *Loneliness : A source book of current theory, research and therapy,* John Wiley, New York.

Purohit, C.K. and Sharma, R., 1973 : A study of aged 60 years and above in social profile, *Indian Journal of Gerontology,* 4, pp. 71-83.

Raja, R.K., 1982 : Problems of the aged, *Yojana,* 26(3), pp. 14-15.

Ranade, S.N., 1985 : 'Social aspects of aging in India', Paper presented at the International Seminar on Population Aging in India, February, Trivandrum.

Randhawa : Maninder and Bhatnagar, G.S., 1985, Changing attitudes and beliefs of the retired people, *Journal of Sociological Studies,* 4, pp. 120-127.

Robert, H. Binstock and Ethel Shanas. (Eds) 1976 : *Handbook of Aging and Social Sciences.* Van Nostrand Reinhold Company, New York.

Ramamurthy, P. V., 1968 : ' A Study of Some Factors Related to the Adjustment of Urban Aged Men' (Unpublished). Doctoral Dissertation, S.V. University, Tirupati.

——,1970 : 'Rigidity, Flexibility in the Older Years'. *Indian Journal of Experimental Psychology,* Vol.4, No. 1.

——,1970 : 'A Study of Certain Socio-Economic Variables Related to Adjustment in Aging'. *Journal of Psychological Research,* Vol. 14.

Ramamurthy, P.V., 1986 : 'Empirically Derived Constitutents for a Happier Old Age'. Paper presented at the Third National Conference on Aging, University of Hyderabad, Hyderabad.

Ramamurthy, P.V. and Jamuna, D., 1987 : 'Psychological Research on the Aged in India'. *Journal of the Indian Anthropological Society,* Vol.20, No.3, Calcutta.

Ranade, S.N., 1974 : 'A Study of the Aged in Delhi. School of Social Work', Delhi. University of Delhi (Mimeographed).

Ranade, S.N., 1985 : 'Social Aspects of Aging in India'. Paper presented at the International Seminar on Population Aging in India, Trivandrum.

Rajan, Irudaya, S., Mishra, U.S., and Sharma, P. Sankara, 1999: *India's Elderly Burden or Challenge,* Sage Publications, New Delhi.

Registrar General of India, 1996 : Census of India 1991. Population Projections for India and States, 1996-2016, Ministry of Home Affairs, Government of India, New Delhi.

Srivastava, Dr. Ram Chandra, 1994 : *The Problem of the Old Age* Classical Publishing Company, New Delhi.

Shah, V.P., 1993 : 'The Elderly in Gujarat' Mimeograph. Department of Sociology, Gujarat University, Ahmedabad.

Sharma, M.L. and T.M. Dak (eds.), 1987 : *Aging in India Challenge for the Society,* Ajanta Publications, New Delhi.

Saraswati Mishra, 1989 : *Social Adjustment in Old Age.* D.K. Publishers Distributors (P) Ltd., New Delhi.

Shanas, E., 1979 : 'The Family as a Social Support System in Old Age'. *Gerontologist,* No.19.

Sharma, M.L. and Dak, T.M., 1982 : *Aging in India Challenge for the Society.* Ajanta Books, New Delhi.

Suresh Chandra, 1970 : 'The Social Challenges of Old Age'. *Social Welfare.* No-17(6) September.

Siddaiah, Marula H.M., 1966 : 'The Declining Authority of Old People.' *Indian Journal of Social Work.* Vol.27, July.

Singh, Amarjit, 1982 : 'Old Age Can be Exciting or Depressing', *Social Welfare*. Vol. XXIX No. 1, April.

Soodan, Kirpal Singh, 1972 : *Aging in India,* Minerva Associates, Calcutta.

Sharma, M.L. and Dak, T.M., 1987, *Aging in India—Challenge for Society,* Ajanta Publication, Delhi.

Singh, J.G., Singh, S. and Dawra, V., 1983 : 'Adjustment problems of old people', *Indian Journal of Clinical Psychology,* 10(1), pp. 127-131.

Tibbitties, Clark (editor) 1960 : *Aging in Society,* University of Chicago Press, Chicago.

Tibbittis, Clark (editor) 1960 : *Handbook of Social Gerontology*, University of Chicago, Chicago.

Tilak, Srinivas, 1989 : *Religion and aging in Indian Tradition,* State University of New York Press, Albany, New York.

Verma, Paripurnanad, 1978 : 'Problems of Aging Adults', *Social Welfare,* Vol. XXV No.2 to 3. May to June.

Vijaya Kumar, S., 1990 : 'Aged in India', New Delhi : The Elderly Forum Vol.V., No. 1

Vijaya, Kumar, S. and Suryanarayana, M., 1986 : 'Gerontology and the Need for a Policy for the Welfare of the Aged', Paper presented at the National Seminar on Relevance of Anthropology Today, Karnataka University, Dharwad.

——, Kumar, S. and Suryanarayana, M., 1986 : 'Family and Social Problems of Retired Employees'. Paper presented at the Third National Conference on Aging, University of Hyderabad, Hyderabad.

——, 1998 : 'Chronological Aging and Consequent Problems', Paper presented at UGC National Seminar on Gerontology, Centre for Research on Aging, S.V. University, Tirupati.

World Health Organization, 1982 : 'Recommendations of the World Health Organization Conference on Aging', W.H.O. Press, New Delhi.

INDEX